Agrarian Reform in
Latin America

Borzoi Books ON LATIN AMERICA

General Editor
LEWIS HANKE
UNIVERSITY OF CALIFORNIA, IRVINE

AGRARIAN REFORM
IN
LATIN AMERICA

❧❧

EDITED WITH AN INTRODUCTORY ESSAY BY

T. Lynn Smith
University of Florida

New York : Alfred·A·Knopf

NOTE: *Documents 14 and 19 are the only selections in this book available heretofore in English. All of the other selections have been newly translated by T. Lynn Smith.*

L. C. catalog card number: 65–11633

THIS IS A BORZOI BOOK

PUBLISHED BY ALFRED A. KNOPF, INC.

FOURTH PRINTING, MAY 1968

This book is dedicated to the memory of
A. P. Figueiredo
and
Salvador Camacho Roldán
far-sighted forerunners of agrarian reform in Latin America

CONTENTS

Part II: Current Agrarian Reform Programs in Latin America

Contents

Agrarian Reform in
Latin America

INTRODUCTION

A General View of Agrarian Reform
Proposals and Programs in
Latin America

❧

Throughout the vast area between the Rio Grande and Cape Horn, among the 240 million inhabitants of the twenty Latin American republics, a cry for "agrarian reform" seems to be the most popular refrain of the day. As one outstanding Brazilian sociologist, educator, and lawyer has written, "never was a *reform* so discussed and debated, in Brazil or outside of it, as the *agrarian*." [1] In Colombia as in Brazil, in Venezuela and Bolivia, in Chile, Costa Rica, and Cuba, in Mexico, Guatemala, Peru, and all the rest fervent discussion of agrarian reform goes on among those high in the social scale, among the increasing numbers of the emerging middle social classes, and among the masses of the population who are of lower-class status. In the press, on radio and television, and in the halls of the national congresses there is a lavish outpouring of words having to do with the need for, the purposes of, and the ways of bringing

---

[1] J. V. Freitas Marcondes, "Reforma Agrária à Luz das Ciências Sociais," *Sociologia* (São Paulo), XXIV, No. 4 (1962), 273.

about changes that are dubbed as agrarian reform. It is true that in some countries, such as Mexico, Bolivia, and Cuba, the past tense is usually used when this all-pervasive topic is mentioned; but neither the universality nor the pitch of the discussion seems to be reduced by that fact.

Under such circumstances politicians at all levels of national life find the call for agrarian reform to be a popular plank for their platforms; demagogues are quick to seize upon this theme in their unceasing endeavors to further their own selfish ends; officials in the ministries of agriculture and other governmental offices find that proposals for changes in the basic relationships of man to the land are among their own chief preoccupations; and social scientists in and out of governmental service recognize that they must give serious attention and study to such subjects as land tenure, the distribution of property rights to the land, the size of the agricultural establishments, and the antiquated systems of agriculture that still prevail in many portions of their countries. In Brazil all of the presidents from 1950 on, that is from Getúlio Vargas to Humberto Castello Branco, have given agrarian reform a high priority in their pronouncements; this has been matched by a similar concern by the chief executives in most of the other Latin American countries. In Mexico, of course, this history goes back to 1910, and was highlighted by the words and actions of such presidents as Portes Gil and Lázaro Cárdenas; but in more recent years the spotlight has turned upon such presidents as the following: Alberto Lleras Camargo of Colombia; Rómulo Betancourt of Venezuela; Víctor Paz Estenssoro of Bolivia; Juan José Arévalo, Jacobo Arbenz, and Manuel Ydígoras of Guatemala; and Juan Bosch of the Dominican Republic. Also in this connection, although he has not chosen to assume the title of President, one merely needs to mention the lip service given by Fidel Castro to the Agrarian Reform Law that was promulgated before he deposed Urrutia as President.

It still is too early to evaluate the ultimate effects of the activities of Castro and associates in firing up the rural masses with the slogan, "the land belongs to the one who tills it," at the same time that they actually were busily engaged in transforming the sugar-cane plantations and other huge estates into state farms patterned on the Soviet models; but there can be no doubt that about 1959 the theme of agrarian reform reached fortissimo pitch in Cuba.

Perhaps, though, the central position of agrarian reform among the host of problems with which Latin America is faced is best expressed by the following words spoken by Dom Helder Câmara, Roman Catholic Archbishop of Rio de Janeiro, in the course of a television broadcast made on February 27, 1963, over a station in Washington, D. C.:

> I am not speaking as a Brazilian addressing Americans but as a man talking to other men [. . .]. The Alliance for Progress is dead, however much I should hope for its resurrection. The main reason for its failure seems to be the following: it was necessary to establish close coordination between the help from the Alliance and the basic reforms, but unfortunately the rich in Latin America talk too much about reform and label as Communists all those who try to enforce it. This is easy to understand: the rich in Latin America go on holding 80 per cent of the land on the Continent. Often they control Parliament and have the intensity of their idealism and hope in the future gauged by the bank deposits kept in their names in the United States and Europe. Unfortunately, the rich in your country also create problems: President Kennedy could be a witness to that.[2]

In brief, the cry for agrarian reform is the dominant note in the loud chorus of discontent that is racking the Spanish American and Brazilian societies during the second half of the twentieth century; and legal and other measures designed to improve man's relationships to the land, endeavors to institute more effective and efficient methods of obtaining crop and animal products, and ways and means for se-

---

[2] From a press release issued by the Brazilian Embassy, Washington, D. C., February 27, 1963.

curing a more equitable distribution of the returns of agricultural enterprises all figure, along with an almost magical belief in industrialization, among the chief hopes of those who are attempting to solve the chronic ills of the various Latin American countries. All of this seems to be true in the camps of those who seek to bring about the development of these nations along the ways of the democratic countries of Western society, and also in the ranks of those who are making every effort to cast the fortunes of all Spanish America and Brazil in with those of Soviet Russia, Communist China, and Castro's Cuba.

In the pages that follow primary attention is given to the following general aspects of the subject, which subsequently are further illustrated by extensive extracts from Latin American sources: the fact that our subject is the broader and more humanistic one of agrarian reform and not the narrower, less accurate, and almost non-Latin American topic of land reform; the development of a concern with agrarian reform in the Latin American countries; the indicators which point to the need for agrarian reform in the various nations under consideration; the major objectives of a program of genuine agrarian reform; and the measures or techniques that are being used or are proposed to bring about substantial progress toward attaining the goals of agrarian reform.

Before proceeding to a discussion of these matters, however, it is well for us to recall that all the Latin American countries except Cuba have solemnly pledged to carry out the various objectives of the Charter of Punta del Este, popularly known as the Alliance for Progress. Prominent among the features of this treaty is number 6 in the list of objectives, which was phrased as follows:

> To encourage, in accordance with the characteristics of each country, programs of comprehensive agrarian reform [note that the expression is *not* land reform] leading to the effective transformation, where required, of unjust structures and systems of land tenure so that, with the help of timely and adequate credit, technical

assistance, and facilities for marketing and distribution of products, the land will become for the man who works it the basis of his economic stability, the foundation of his increasing welfare, and the guarantee of his freedom and dignity.

Moreover, all of the countries subscribed to the provisions embodied in Title II, Chapter II, Section 2, paragraph d of the Charter, which indicates that "National development programs should incorporate self-help efforts directed to: [. . .] the more effective, rational and equitable mobilization and use of financial resources through the reform of tax structures, including fair and adequate taxation of large incomes and real estate." Finally, and without this any proposed agrarian reform would be little more than a mockery, the countries committed themselves (in Title I, 7) "to eliminate adult illiteracy and by 1970 to assure, as a minimum, access to six years of primary education to every child in Latin America."

AGRARIAN REFORM OR LAND REFORM?

The reader will note, of course, that this volume is devoted to *agrarian reform* and not to *land reform*. This choice was made deliberately, and it was made despite the fact that in the United States the latter expression is employed with far greater frequency than the former by those who speak or write about proposals for remodeling the institutional features of agriculture and rural life. Nevertheless, the reasons for the choice are simple. This small book is concerned with Latin America; therefore one must stress that in all of the Spanish American countries and also in Brazil one may encounter only now and then an article or an address which has a title indicating that it is on the subject of the *problema de la tierra,* or its Portuguese equivalent. Generally these have little or nothing to do with any frame of reference related to agrarian reform. As a matter of fact, if one were to speak or write about *la reforma de la tierra* or *a reforma da terra* almost inevitably anyone attend-

ing to his words would gain the impression that some physical remaking of the earth's surface, such as that involved in
terracing or leveling, was the matter involved. There is, of
course, no agreement among the Latin Americans of various
ideologies and distinct political hues with respect to the
content of measures designed to change the relationships of
man to the land, but on one point they all seem to be in accord: irrespective of the nature of the changes they are discussing or advocating, the name for them is the *reforma
agraria*. This alone is sufficient reason for the choice of titles that we have made.

It is well to indicate, however, that even more than this
is involved. The vast majority of the proposals made ver-
bally or in writing, and especially the drafts of the proposed
laws dealing with agrarian reform, include far more than
measures designed to bring about changes in the land tenure
system or to modify the *régimen de las tierras*. This will be
abundantly clear to those who read the extracts presented
in this book, which were selected to show the nature of the
problem and the proposed solutions in the various countries. Thus, in Bolivia the problem of the Indian figures
alongside that of tenure and the size of the estates; in Brazil the valorization of the common rural Brazilian is a primary concern; in Colombia the development of a genuine
middle social class of farmers has long been and continues
to be a fundamental concern of those attempting to modify
the institutional structures of Colombia's agriculture and
nowadays *acción comunal* (or community development)
also looms large in the picture; and those phrasing and pro-
mulgating Cuba's Agrarian Reform Law (which was presented in its English text as the Land Reform Law!) were
primarily concerned with the disadvantages of large-scale
agriculture and the ownership of land by foreigners.

For almost a decade now I have been lecturing and pub-
lishing widely throughout all portions of Latin America and
in the United States on the subject of agrarian reform. In
the course of this period I have met and conversed with
hundreds of those who should be most conversant with the
subject in all countries from Mexico to Argentina and Chile,

as well as in all parts of the United States; and I have read and studied hundreds of articles, speeches, monographs, books, and laws or proposed laws on the subject. From this, two impressions stand out above all others in my mind: (1) in Latin America there is the utmost diversity in the content of the thought that collectively is denoted as agrarian reform; and (2) in the United States a great many people appear to have almost a psychosis against anything that carries the title of agrarian reform or land reform.

Probably throughout both Latin America and the United States the most widespread meaning attached to the topic would define agrarian reform or land reform as the seizing of the land held in large estates, dividing it into very small plots, and distributing the latter among the agricultural wage hands and other types of farm laborers. Sometimes in this type of thinking, particularly in some of the Latin American countries, the land involved would be limited largely to idle lands which presently are rather deliberately withheld from productive uses (the *latifundismo* of countries such as Brazil and Colombia), and with considerable frequency that which is tilled by various kinds of sharecroppers or share tenants would be the first target. The extent to which the owners would be remunerated and the manner in which this would be done also differ widely.

In practice one rarely hears or reads proposals along these lines, except in the subterranean endeavors made in personal contacts with the *campesinos* by those seeking to weld them into a solid block of support for a proposed new order, or in the speeches made by "firebrands" to gatherings of the same humble portions of the Latin American population. The intellectuals of Marxist leanings always proclaim increased agricultural production to be the principal objective; apparently they would much prefer to preserve the large estates intact so that they might easily and quickly be transformed into state farms, without the necessity of dispossessing once more any portion of the rural masses that might have gotten control of the land. Those who are not dominated by the Marxist ideologies, including many Socialists who deplore Marx's abysmal ignorance of agriculture and rural life, are split into the proponents of various radically differing lines of action, of which by far the most important is that of getting the ownership of the land into the hands of a genuine middle class of farmers. This point will be developed below, but at this moment, and as further indication of the logic of the title Agrarian Reform, the following comments seem to be in order.

As the history of Haiti so abundantly demonstrates, any reform which involves nothing more than the confiscation of the large estates and their subsequent redistribution in small plots to the farm laborers is almost sure to prove disappointing to nearly everyone concerned. It is certain to bring about a sharp reduction in agricultural production and greatly worsen the national situation. Individually the rural families are somewhat better off, but unaided by education, credit institutions, and so on, even they cannot rise substantially above the creature level of existence which previously was their lot. This is because the active element in the man-land equation is the worker or peasant himself, not the land. What is done with him, by him, and for him and his family will certainly determine in the long run, and probably even in the short run, the success or failure of any agrarian or land reform program. To make a farmer of the agricultural laborer requires much more than giving or selling him 5, 10, 50, 100, or 500 acres of land. In the personality of the farmer are combined the execution of all three of the basic economic functions, that is those of the person who saves and invests modest amounts of capital, those of the manager, and those of the laborer. The kind of farmer envisioned in most of the agrarian reform projects throughout Latin America is one who will receive a part of his income from the investment he has in land, livestock, and equipment; a part of it as a reward for the interminable hours he spends in planning and executing the details of management over the enterprises he carries on; and a part of it as a wage for the labor performed by himself and the members of his family.

Where, as throughout most of Latin America, the large estate has been for centuries the nucleus of the social and agricultural system in vogue, it may seem difficult to effect any substantial program for bringing about a more widespread distribution of land ownership. However, that task is merely child's play in comparison with the one of developing the necessary managerial skills on the part of the heads of families whose only roles previously have been the limited ones of the agricultural laborer. The fact that the Latin Americans almost universally speak of agrarian reform and not of land reform is at least a tacit recognition that much more is involved in the solution of the chronic and acute ills than a mere land redistribution program. They know that the major challenge is that of transforming the ordinary rural man into a being much nearer the human potential than he presently is.

The approach of some of the more able Latin Americans to the subject, and a clear indication of why the phenomenon cannot logically be denoted as land reform, is exemplified by the following extracts from the paper "Conceituação da Reforma Agrária," which Gustavo Corção prepared for the Simpósio sobre Reforma Agrária organized by the Instituto Brasileiro de Ação Democrática in Rio de Janeiro in 1961:

> For us agrarian reform is not essentially a change in the regime of property; but also it cannot be realized without such a change, as is evident in the publication entitled "Land Reform" issued in English by the United Nations on July 23, 1951.
>
> The distribution of property in land, although not the essence of nor the central objective of a good agrarian reform, is one of the factors involved in it. This problem of a better distribution of the land, in turn, falls between a solution that is uniform and general and another which, because of its exaggerated plasticity, destroys all the efficacy of the reform. Genuine agrarian reform is pluralistic, and will have a place for various types of what the English text of the United Nations publication calls land tenure. Having in view the creation of a rural middle class, an agrarian reform

should lean strongly toward a regime of properties distributed according to this criterion [. . .].

In résumé, the concept of an agrarian reform of the democratic type is as follows: it is a group of political, cultural, and economic measures which should be applied wherever are to be observed the signs (a), (b), (c), (d), etc., indicators of a defective agrarian structure and causes of a subhuman condition of life. This group of measures should seek the immediate elevation of the human level and the dignification of the rural populations; it should also seek, as a consequence of this, the general improvement of the political, cultural, and economic level of the people among whom it is applied.

Many of the writings of V. M. Giménez Landínez, Minister of Agriculture in Venezuela, also illustrate the inadequacy of the expression "land reform" as a translation of the Latin American "agrarian reform." For example, in the exposition he prepared for the First International Catholic Rural Life Conference, held at Rome in September, 1962, there are several explicit statements of the fact that agrarian reform is a much broader concept than land reform. One of these which is sufficient for present purposes is as follows:

Agrarian reform is, in effect, quite a distinct thing, more complex and more profound, from this simple aspect of the distribution of land conceived of at times by an already decrepit revolutionism. Also it is more than the convenience of giving the ownership of the land to the campesino so as to tie him to the soil and increase production, because he invests more, as some think. Agrarian reform is much more than this: it is based in the *right* of the man who tills the soil that this shall be useful for his welfare and independence; so that the concept must include, in addition to the land problem itself, that of credit to enable him to work the soil and that of the security of markets to make it truly productive.

But still more is involved. In the Tenth World Congress of the Food and Agriculture Organization, held here in Rome in November 1959, we said that if agrarian reform were considered merely as one simple aspect of development (that is, taking account only of what it might signify in the tenure structure or in increased productivity), it would never acquire the stature nor the elevation with which it is understood and felt in the language of the people because, at least in our Latin American countries, it has always been understood and sensed as a symbol and banner. And I added that, in order to attain this category, agrarian reform needed and must have the most solid juridical bases.[3]

BACKGROUND OF THE CURRENT OUTBURST OF INTEREST IN AGRARIAN REFORM

If one reflects about the timing of the current outcry for agrarian reform throughout Latin America he well may wonder why the outburst came early in the second half of the twentieth century and not about 1800, 1850, 1900, 1920, or even 1940. As will be evident from what is said below, if judged by present standards and values, most of the indicators of the need for substantial agrarian reform programs have been present for centuries, and able proponents of substantial changes in the distribution of landownership and other aspects of the prevailing social systems have appeared from time to time. Nevertheless, for the most part prior to 1950 the advocates of agrarian reform measures did not succeed in bringing to a feverish pitch the dissatisfaction and discontent of the rural masses in the immense areas which lay between the Rio Grande and Cape Horn.

Neither the revolutionary forces from outside the hemisphere nor those which brought profound changes and reforms within certain nations of the New World made a general impression throughout Latin America. Thus, late in the eighteenth century when Haiti carried through a drastic agrarian reform involving the complete elimination of the

[3] V. M. Giménez Landínez, *Agricultura, Reforma Agraria y Desarrollo* (Caracas: Editorial Arte, 1962), pp. 50-51.

landowning master class, the freeing of the slaves, and a thorough-going redistribution of ownership rights to the land, there was no tendency for other countries to follow suit, even though the movements for independence were getting under way at the time and revolts were soon to break out. Likewise, more than a century later, when the deep-cutting Mexican agrarian revolution took place, there appear to have been relatively few repercussions in the other Latin American countries. In all probability most of the Latin Americans who were cognizant of the Haitian and Mexican upheavals considered them as horrible examples of what should be avoided at all cost rather than as developments that should be imitated. The fact is that even in the opening quarter of the twentieth century drastic changes such as those taking place in Mexico had little appeal to the members of the upper classes in other parts of Latin America, a small group who owned the land, controlled the government and the economy, and managed the means of communication; while the huge masses of agricultural laborers, still in a servile or semi-servile condition, un-schooled and almost hermetically sealed off from all contacts and influences other than those within their own immediate surroundings, never even knew that there was a bloody struggle for "land and liberty" going on in a country called Mexico. Similarly the agrarian reforms, or "Green Rising," which swept Europe soon after the close of the First World War seem to have had little or no immediate impact upon the Latin American countries.

The fact is, of course, that even as late as 1920 contacts between Latin Americans and their fellows in other parts of the world were extremely limited, and the Spanish Americans and Brazilians who participated in these consisted largely of members of the affluent families who had the desire and the funds necessary to travel abroad. At that time, in sharp contrast with the situation after 1950, there were no large contingents of Latin American students in European and North American universities; the airplane, radio, and automobile were of practically no significance in the contacts of persons in one country with those in another, and television had hardly been dreamed of; international organizations and agencies were not bringing about annually the visits of thousands of Latin American specialists and technicians to other sections of the world, nor flooding the Latin American countries with professional people from abroad; and the concerted efforts of organized ideological groups to change the status quo in the various countries were merely in their beginning stages. In brief, the factors that soon were to produce the contacts needed in order to confront Latin American standards and values with those prevailing elsewhere were only beginning to have an impact. Therefore, even in 1920 it was possible for a social system based largely upon feudalistic patterns and values to persist almost without challenge throughout the rural portions of most parts of Latin America.

Before proceeding with this analysis it appears desirable to comment briefly upon the two principal social systems which give organization and meaning to rural societies or the rural portions of those societies in which the urban population forms a significant portion of the total. One of these highly integrated entities has as its core the large landed estate; the other is one in which a wide distribution of land ownership and control prevails and in which the family-sized farm unit is the principal determinant of life and labor in the rural districts. Each of these central features gives rise to and perpetuates other essential features and characteristics of the social system which prevails in the society in which it is dominant. Thus, where the large estate rules supreme, society inevitably comes to be divided into two widely separated social classes: a small landowning elite at a very high level in the social scale and, far below, the large mass of the population who function merely in the menial roles of agricultural laborers and generally are doomed to an existence that is very little above the mere creature level. All this is very different in the society in which family-sized farms are in the hands of the vast majority of those who live by cultivating the soil. In such a society the middle class is the dominant feature of the social pyramid, and there is little or nothing resembling a landowning elite, on the one hand, or any substantial number of permanent lower-class agricultural laborers, on the other.

In like manner, the large estate brings into existence and perpetuates a large number of other highly important features of the social system in the areas it dominates, of which the following may be mentioned in summary form: (1) a low degree of vertical social mobility; (2) a strong element of caste, or the tendency for the social position of the offspring to be determined by that of their parents; (3) low average levels of intelligence among the agricultural population; (4) restricted development of the personalities of the mass of the population, for the agricultural laborers never have the opportunity to develop many of their human potentialities; (5) relationships of the "order and obey" type, or domination and subordination, between the members of the upper class and those who belong among the masses; (6) a high value placed upon routine, with the workers not expected to, or even not permitted to depart from the endless repetition under the watchful eyes of an overseer of a few elementary activities required by the monoculture in which they are involved; (7) work with the hands, manual labor of any type, is considered degrading and is shunned as the plague by all who are in a position to do so; (8) low average levels and standards of living; and (9) very little stimulus to regular work activities and habits of thrift and saving.

All of these are quite different in the social system of which the family-sized farm pattern forms the core. There, farmers of middle-class status make up the bulk of the population, a middle-class mentality prevails, and social stratification is reduced to a minimum. A high degree of mobility, or the shifting of persons up and down the limited range of the social scale, goes on with little hindrance, so that the caste element is largely lacking. In such a rural society the average intelligence of the rural population is high, and each agriculturist engages directly in the performance of all three of the economic functions (those of the investor of capital, of the manager, and of the laborer) and teaches his children competence in the same. Relationships run strongly to the equalitarian type, and the role of leadership contrasts sharply with the ordering and forbidding that obtains in the system that prevails in districts given over to plantations or other large landed estates. In the family-sized farm system the search for the new, the improved, everything that will save labor and improve efficiency, is the general rule. Therefore, it is no accident that practically all of the world's modern agricultural implements and machines were invented and perfected in the family-sized farming districts of Europe and the United States. Furthermore, in this system, manual labor is considered uplifting and dignifying, levels and standards of living tend to be high, and there is the maximal stimulus to steady work habits and attitudes of thrift and saving.

That the dominant social system in the rural portions of Latin America historically has been and continues to be that based upon the large landed estate is so well known as to require no documentation in this treatise. Innumerable writers have pointed out its most distinguishing features, such as: (1) a two-class system in which the wealth, power, and prestige are monopolized by a small number of elite families who occupy the apex of the social scale; the bulk of the people (the natives, the imported slaves, and the descendants of both) are relegated to the bottom of the social pyramid in one large mass of lower-class status; (2) a situation in which the princely position of the masters is based upon the ownership and control of huge landed estates on which the masses toil in order to subsist and with little or no reason to hope for an improvement in their own lot or that of their children; and (3) all the power and all the amenities of life are the exclusive right of the members of the few upper-class families. In brief, the traditional social system of the Latin American societies and the values which gave it consistency and meaning are those that would assist in establishing and defending the ethical rightness of a highly stratified society and give sanction to the behavior of the members of the upper classes. Many of these, of course, were considered archaic, feudalistic, and intolerable when Latin American societies were suddenly thrust into considerable contact with others in the "Century of the Common Man." In Brazil, for example, prior to 1940 unrestrained praise of the large estate, such as the following widely published statement by an outstanding lawyer and sociologist, seemed to arouse no adverse criticism whatsoever:

> In our country [. . .] agriculture had its beginning in the large estate. The Romans evolved the large property from the small [. . .]. Other peoples developed it in a similar manner. In contrast with this, we have been from the beginning a nation of latifundia: among us the history of the small farm can be said to go back only a century. All the long colonial period was one of the splendor of the immense territorial property. In this period it alone appeared and shined; it alone created and dominated; it is the central theme interwoven throughout the entire drama of our history for three hundred fecund and glorious years.[4]

From 1950 on, though, it would be difficult if not impossible to find any writer of consequence who has risen to the defense of the latifundia. Indeed, as far as can be ascertained in all of Latin America there have been no publications whatsoever which glorify the large estate in a manner at all comparable with the praises heaped upon it by Oliveira Vianna. Universally, latifundio and latifundista seem to have acquired highly opprobrious connotations. The rapid change in values, of which this example is illustrative, has been, in the last analysis, responsible for the timing of the sudden outburst of interest in agrarian reform throughout Latin America.

In this examination of some of the background of the current interest in agrarian reform throughout Latin America it must be stressed that in the long period between independence and 1950 there were important instances in which the necessity for such reform was recognized and measures for bringing it about were proposed. However, just as the in-

---

[4] F. J. Oliveira Vianna, "O Povo Brazileiro e sua Evolução." *Recenseamento do Brazil, 1920*, Vol. I (Rio de Janeiro: Imprensa Nacional, 1922), p. 282.

fluences from Haiti, Mexico, and Europe failed to make an impression upon the activities of the leaders in most of the countries, the local stirrings failed to spread widely within the countries in which they developed. To take stock of such developments in all the Latin American nations would require years of intensive research on the social and agrarian history of each of the countries; it is a task that has not been done and one that is far beyond the scope of this volume.[5] The remainder of this section, therefore, is devoted to developments in Brazil and Colombia, the two countries to which I have devoted a major portion of my time for more than a quarter of a century. It should be mentioned, though, that Brazil alone makes up more than one third of Latin America, and Colombia occupies what may be thought of as a middle position among the eighteen Spanish American republics.

In Brazil, sporadic outbursts of concern relative to defective relationships between man and the land dot that country's entire history as an independent nation. This history began in 1822, and this was exactly the time when Gonçalves Chaves, writing anonymously, described existing conditions in the following terms, an analysis which one authority (Ruy Cirne Lima) states has never been excelled:

1. Our population is almost nothing in comparison with the immensity of the territory which we have already occupied for three centuries.

2. The lands are almost all divided and there are few, except those subject to invasion by Indians, left to distribute.

---

[5] For some of the countries the interested reader can find substantial pertinent information in the following works listed in the Bibliography pp. 195-206: Carl C. Taylor, *Rural Life in Argentina*; Olen E. Leonard, *Bolivia: Land, People and Institutions*; T. Lynn Smith, *Brazil: People and Institutions*; G. M. McBride, *Chile: Land and Society*; Orlando Fals Borda, *Hombre y Tierra en Boyacá*; Lowry Nelson, *Rural Cuba*; Nathan L. Whetten, *Guatemala: The Land and the People*; G. M. McBride, *The Land Systems of Mexico*; Eyler N. Simpson, *The Ejido: Mexico's Way Out*; Frank Tannenbaum, *The Mexican Agrarian Revolution*; Nathan L. Whetten, *Rural Mexico*; and Thomas R. Ford, *Man and Land in Peru*.

3. The monopolists possess up to 20 leagues of land and rare are the times that they consent for any family to establish itself on any part of their lands, and even when they do consent, it is always temporarily and never by contract which would permit the family to remain several years.

4. There are many poor families wandering from place to place, following the favor and caprice of land-owners and always lacking the means of obtaining some ground on which they could establish themselves permanently.

5. Our agriculture is as backward and unprogressive as is possible among any agricultural people, even the least advanced in civilization.[6]

Another interesting example of concern with the basic elements of agrarian reform developed in Pernambuco about the middle of the nineteenth century. This was expressed in the writings of A. P. Figueiredo, whose analysis is second to none, and whose works figure prominently in the translations prepared for use in this volume (see Documents 1, 2, and 3). Figueiredo was strongly influenced by the ideas of European Socialists, such as Fourier, St. Simon, Owen, and Buchez, and he was analyzing and prescribing for the ills of the sugar-producing districts of the northeast, the section which continues to be the Problem Area Number 1 of Brazil. Anyone seriously interested in the backgrounds of agrarian reform measures in Brazil would do well to peruse the articles he wrote for Recife newspapers, the speeches he made at political rallies, and the articles he wrote for the review, O Progresso, which he edited. Even though his diagnoses and prescriptions did not gain widespread acceptance at the time, they demonstrate that the problems of agriculture and rural life in this portion of Brazil were already both chronic and acute and that they were not essen-

---

[6] Translated from the extracts presented in Ruy Cirne Lima, *Terras Devolutas* (Porto Alegre: Livraria do Globo, 1935), pp. 43-44.

tially different about 1850 than they were a century later. Among the matters to which he devoted attention, as may be seen from the extracts from his works which are presented later in this volume, the following deserve special attention: (1) the pitiful living conditions of the masses of the population; (2) the stagnation of agriculture; (3) concentration of landownership and control as the factor chiefly responsible for the unsatisfactory state of affairs; (4) political and administrative procedures that made a mockery of democratic or republican institutions; (5) the necessity of developing a middle social class of family-sized farmers; and (6) the use of the general property tax as a principal technique for accomplishing the reforms needed and proposed.

Less than twenty years after Figueiredo wrote so accurately and so lucidly on the topics that are central to any genuine program of agrarian reform, many of his conclusions were generalized for Brazil in a noteworthy report prepared for that country's Minister of Agriculture. After describing the lavish manner in which huge portions of the public domain had been conferred upon a few highly favored persons, this report goes on to say:

> As a result of this amplitude of liberty all the lands about the cities and important villages on the coast fell into private ownership, so that today it is not possible to find near the populous cities, close to the markets, or along the main lines of communication a single palm of land belonging to the State that could be converted into a nucleus of a colony or distributed to immigrants. Since the owners lack the means for cultivating such vast expanses of land, much of it remains uncultivated and without villages or houses.
>
> Out of this concentration of property in the hands of a few comes the abandonment of agriculture in the rural districts, the stagnation or lack of development in urban construction, the poverty and dependency of a large part of the population, who can find no field for their activity nor means to become proprietors, and,

finally, the difficulties that prevent the administration from offering a commodious and appropriate location to immigrants.[7]

In the course of the next decade, during the height of the Abolition Campaign, other writers and orators were proclaiming similar ideas, but once the slaves were freed (1888), for the most part these ideas faded from the picture. Then, for over half a century, while Brazilian cities were growing and her industries were being established and developed, "Brazilian agriculture and the Brazilian countryside remained bound, by feudalistic forms of society and economy, to ways of doing and thinking characteristic of the pre-capitalistic era in which they originated." [8]

The backgrounds of current agrarian reform proposals and programs in the Spanish American countries differ substantially from those in Brazil, and, especially after independence was secured, the developments in every country were considerably different from those in each of the others. As indicated above, the materials included here are limited to those for Colombia. As in the other sections of Spanish America, however, during the colonial period the two-class social system based upon the large landed estate was the essential feature of Colombian society. Throughout the long colonial epoch the lavish granting of large and ill-defined tracts of land, the failure to provide for systematic surveys, carelessness in the recording of titles, and occasional legalization of illegal claims established a pattern from which the nation continues to suffer acutely. As a matter of fact, less than a century after the conquest the relations of man to the land in what is now Colombia were already in a chaotic condition. In this early part of the colonial period, the only legal manner of alienating public lands was through grants or gifts by the King or his representatives, including the lo-

[7] João Cardoso de Menezes e Souza, *Theses sôbre Colonização no Brasil* (Rio de Janeiro: Typográphia Nacional, 1875), pp. 153-154.

[8] José Arthur Rios, in the Introduction to the volume edited by him, *Recomendações sôbre Reforma Agrária* (Rio de Janeiro: Instituto Brasileiro de Ação Democrática, 1961), p. xii.

cal *cabildo,* or council. But the colonists were not content with these gifts, even though one may well be surprised at the liberality with which some of the conquistadores were given one large grant after another; they seem to have resorted to all kinds of expedients to supplement the areas to which they were legally entitled. In some cases the landowners merely occupied and claimed extensions of territory greatly in excess of those specified in their concessions; in others it appears that they had titles bestowed by persons who had no authority to represent the King; and in still others forgeries were used in the concoction of completely fraudulent titles. As time passed many of the proprietary rights, legal and otherwise, changed hands several times, so that large numbers of persons, in perfectly good faith, were holding lands to which the titles were defective. In an attempt to correct this situation, the King, in 1591, issued the noted *Cedulas del Pardo* which provided for the *Composición,* or regularization, of claims to land in the colony. This resulted in an endeavor to judge each claim in the light of the special circumstances surrounding it. It had the effect of regaining for the Crown extensive tracts of land that had been held illegally, but it also provided valid titles to many claimants whose deeds to the claims had been defective.

The reforms, though, failed to have any lasting effect. The members of the powerful upper class continued to help themselves liberally to those portions of the public domain which they desired. Furthermore, this process of getting the bulk of the land into the hands of a few and of keeping the control of it there was greatly promoted by the work of some of the religious organizations. In Colombia, as in most other parts of Spanish America, during colonial times the priests were the chief champions of the Indians' rights to personal freedom and the continued possession of the lands they were using at the time of the conquest. Had it not been for them very few of the Indians would have escaped actual enslavement. In spite of this, church institutions themselves came to be one of the principal factors in bringing about an accumulation of huge expanses of landed property under a single ownership; and since the *mayorazgos*, or entailed estates, were not abolished until 1824, they helped perpetuate the system of large estates for many years after the control of them had passed to other hands. Thus, for example, even the partial data that are available seem to indicate that the Jesuits alone, before their expulsion in 1767, had consolidated many already large holdings into more than 100 tremendous estates.[9] In brief, the evidence leaves no doubt that a considerable number of the *haciendas* which today monopolize large expanses of Colombia's most fertile lands were originally put together as large estates by religious organizations. Consider, for example, the explicit statements of Antonio Manso, President of the Audiencia of the Nuevo Reino de Granada, in his report for the year 1729:

I have reserved for the conclusion of this report another of the most universal causes of the poverty of the Kingdom and its inhabitants, one so difficult to remove that to the powerful arm of Your Majesty alone is reserved its remedy. It is, my Lord, that the piety of the faithful in these parts is excessive; it has enriched the monasteries and the orders with various gifts, pious works which establish in the churches *capellanías* [trust funds to pay for masses, and so forth] which are given for the use of the order; many persons finding themselves without legal heirs have established with a small house, a lot, or a small farm a capellanía for this or that convent; and with these and their industry the orders have built up riches with which they have purchased large haciendas. Next they loaned their funds to the people of the community at the honest rate of 5 per cent, taking as security a mortgage on the borrower's house or hacienda; and if some time passed without the interest and principal being paid the mortgage was foreclosed and the property passed into the

---

[9] *Cf.* José Joaquín Borda, *Historia de la Compañía de Jesús en la Nueva Granada,* Vol. II (Poissy: S. LeJay et Cie., 1872), pp. 136-140; and for what amounts virtually to a life history of one of these estates, see Carlos Rodríguez Maldonado, *Hacienda de Tena (IV Centenario)* 1543-1943 (Bogotá: Editorial El Gráfico, 1944).

hands of the convent; in this manner the owners have come to work to pay interest to the convents; and gradually all the valuable properties have been made into church lands [. . .] since that which does not belong to some convent is owned by some secular clergyman who has established a capellanía there.[1]

Little or no improvement in the distribution of ownership and control of the land accompanied the establishment of the Republic, for then:

Unoccupied or "baldío" lands were portioned out in payment for services in the cause of independence, and the same was done as recompense to the legitimist chiefs of the war of 1840. To the grants of the Monarchy were added the feudal concessions of the Republic.[2] Thus the land remained unused in the hands of a few owners, withheld from clearing and planting, in vast latifundia which, in their day, were a new obstacle to the expansion and progress of the agricultural zone.

The region between the Cauca and the Atrato, for example, all belonged to a few capitalists. The district which lies between the Pozo and the Chinchina belonged to a single proprietor, and that was the rule. The virgin forest was preserved intact, protected by titles and concessions, while the cultivated or arable land was insufficient to feed the population.

On the other hand, the people without habitual work were caught on the prongs of the "vagrancy laws," severely applied from 1840 on. The consequence? The great masters, the large landowners of Medellín and

---

[1] The report from which this extract has been translated is reprinted in E. Posada and P. M. Ibáñez, *Relaciones de Mando* (Bogotá: Imprenta Nacional, 1910), p. 13.

[2] The grants of land as payment for services in the cause of independence were not limited to previously unoccupied or undeveloped areas. The first President and Vice President, Bolívar and Santander, for example, jointly received the Hacienda of Tena, to which reference is made above, as partial payment for their services. [Ed.]

Antioquia, filled their labor gangs with persons accused of vagrancy and used them to clear the jungles of the Cauca Valley, so that, without the incentive of property ownership, these unpaid colonists found themselves compelled to contribute their labor under pain of falling under the majesty of the law.[3]

It follows almost as the night follows the day that such a system of large estates would develop and perpetuate the entire set of social, economic, and political ills that contemporary leaders are trying to correct by means of a substantial agrarian reform. This is true despite the fact that to an occasional visitor life on some of the baronial estates may have appeared to be fairly idyllic, if one may judge by early descriptions such as the following:

April 8th [1823]. Left Villeta at 9, A.M., arrived Guaduas—four leagues, at 1, P.M. Parts of the road very steep—enjoyed some fine views.

We presented letters from our friends in Bogotá to Colonel Acosta, who entertained us very hospitably. This gentleman is the Juez-político of the village of Guaduas, and proprietor of thirty leagues square of mountainous, but fruitful land. He is a well-informed, agreeable man, of patriarchal simplicity of manners. In one end of his large house, he keeps a store, containing some foreign fabrics, and the little manufacture of his tenants; principally consisting of straw hats, which are manufactured in almost every house in the village, sandals, baskets, and wooden vessels. He attends to this little shop himself. While sitting with him here, I had an opportunity of witnessing the kind interest he took, as a magistrate and landlord, in the affairs of his clients and tenants, as well as their respectful, yet confiding, bearing in his presence. These tenants pay from six to eight and ten dollars per annum for as much land as

---

[3] Ramón Franco R., *Anthropogeografía Colombiana* (Manizales: Imprenta del Departamento, 1941), pp. 178-179.

they choose to cultivate. We saw some of them, who came to barter with their patron, dispose of their manufactures, obtain a small loan, and ask alms or advice. They were all kindly received, listened to with patience, and dismissed contented.[4]

A century later, however, it would have been difficult, if not impossible, to find examples of such Arcadian bliss. By 1920 the disastrous effects of the large estates and the two-class social system were apparent to many. Consider, for example, the analysis and description of some of these effects as they have been presented by one eminent Colombian political economist:

The existence of the privileged landed class has not merely had the effect of almost depopulating the land adjacent to the principal routes of communication [. . .] but it has had a disastrous moral and political effect upon the less capacitated part of the population residing on these feudal estates. We have studied calmly and without the spirit of controversy the state of affairs which the existence of these enormous tracts of land controlled by a single proprietor have created or provoked in Boyacá, Tolima, Bolívar, and, on a smaller scale, in Antioquia and Santander. The people living on these latifundia vegetate in a strange land, lacking the inclination and activity that are inspired by life and work on one's own property; they lead a migratory existence, exposed to every condition and contingency, like the Gypsies of the Balkan countries. All of us know that one of the conditions imposed upon them expressly or tacitly is that of voting in the popular assemblies for the candidate favored by the proprietor. This strikes at the very foundation of the Republic, although it is a phenomenon that is passed over without comment,

---

[4] Richard Bache, *Notes on Colombia* (Philadelphia: H. C. Carey & I. Lea, 1827), p. 245. See also, William Leay, *New Granada, Equatorial South America* (London: Christian Book Society, 1869), p. 102.

for, in reality, the owners of the latifundia are invested with a plurality of votes.

Equally noxious for national unity and the preservation of peace in the nation is the existence of this population, nomadic, wandering, discontented, lacking roots in the soil in which it vegetates, and, propelled by an unconscious thirst for revenge, neither well defined nor concrete, ready to spring into revolt at the call of the first politician who appeals to their worst instincts in the name of abstract causes. How many times has the revolutionary chieftain set forth with his proclamation with his own laborers as his soldiers! This state of things has produced the abjection among the lower classes of Boyacá, and a rebellion so fearful among them in Tolima that only those who observed on the spot the war of the guerrillas of 1900 are able to appreciate it.[5]

Even more enlightening in many ways are the comments upon the system as it affected the lives of those on his own estate and the haciendas of his neighbors by what must be considered one of the better representatives of the old order. These were published in 1944 in a volume which was prepared in true baronial style to celebrate the four hundredth anniversary of the founding of the Hacienda of Tena. At this time the hacienda included, in addition to the facilities for processing coffee, manufacturing sugar, and some sawmills, "various spacious and modern buildings known by the names of *Mon Repos, Mon Plaisir, Mon Tresor, Mignón, Desiree, Beau Sejour, Micheline, Zoilo-Emilia, Petits Plaisirs,* and others of less importance." [6] This list does not include the old colonial mansion which once was a retreat for Bolívar and Santander. In view of the fact that in 1944 the portion of Colombia in which the Tena Hacienda is located was ablaze with conflicts involving the *colonos,* or

---

[5] Alejandro López, *Problemas Colombianos* (Paris: Editorial Paris-America, 1927), pp. 58-59.

[6] Rodríguez Maldonado, *op. cit.,* p. 149.

squatters, it is interesting that the master of this great estate would comment that "I have had the good fortune of having no problem whatsoever with the more than 250 *arrendatarios,* healthy workers, whom I have considered my friends." [7] Even more enlightening for present purposes, however, is the following "testament" with which he concluded his book:

In spite of the fact that the majority of my two hundred arrendatarios on my Hacienda de Tena are illiterate and unable to read my imprudent words, I wish to leave evidence of my loving gratitude to all of these humble campesinos, collaborators whom I have considered as friends, and not as slaves.

I have undertaken to understand with a humanitarian spirit their sentiments, respected their plantings, listened to all of their troubles, rendered assistance to them occasionally, and satisfied their last desire: a coffin of wood emanating from the same soil on which they were born, worked, suffered, and which we shall all enjoy some day, rich and poor, eternally, unlimitedly.

Hence my inability to understand those *hacendados* who have accused their colonos of taking everything from dry sticks to the fruit which they have lost, who have established tolls on the interior trails and levied tribute upon the produce harvested through sweat and constant privation. All of these owners of rural estates have harvested the fruits of their avarice.

It gives me great satisfaction to declare publicly that none of my employees, workers, peons, or arrendatarios has caused me any mortification. On the contrary, without exception they have given proof of sincere affection. All of them have complied fully with their rental agreements on the parcels of land of my property, without any impediment whatever in the way of their complete enjoyment of their plantings and improvements.

---

[7] *Ibid.,* p. 157.

In respecting their rights they have respected my own.[8]

One should not fail to mention that there were in Colombia during the nineteenth century some substantial attempts at colonization, of which the spontaneous movement of the *Antioqueños* to the south and their blanketing of the Department of Caldas with family-sized farms is by far the most important.[9] For the most part, however, it was an epoch in which population was slight in relation to the available land, political uprisings and civil wars were frequent, and the vast majority of the humble rural folk were unaware of the rights which they might demand under the constitution. Accordingly, other than the southward movement of the Antioqueños, there seem to have been relatively few forces making for any substantial changes in the nature of property rights to the land and the manner in which these rights were distributed among the population. We may be sure, however, that all during this century in various parts of the Republic, more and more families of campesinos were discovering the possibility of avoiding the payment of rent and gaining relative freedom by settling down on small tracts of ground and opening subsistence farms in the forests. We may also be sure that the proprietors of extensive estates were allowing the limits of their haciendas to overlap adjacent territories so that the boundaries of their claims would come to extend far beyond those to which their legal documents gave them ownership rights.

During the opening quarter of the twentieth century the problem that had been building up came to a head, foreshadowing the dramatic events that would characterize the second and third quarters of the century. Before the First World War was over a rapidly increasing population was pressing hard upon the carrying capacity of the land resources in the inhabited parts of the Republic. The fact that severe erosion was rapidly washing the economic basis for

---

[8] *Ibid.*, p. 231.

[9] *Cf.* James J. Parsons, *Antioqueño Colonization in Western Colombia* (Berkeley: University of California Press, 1949).

subsistence from beneath large rural populations helped to accentuate the problems.[1] Hundreds of thousands found it difficult to know which way to turn, and many of them tried to solve their problems by squatting on unused portions of the extensive estates which blanketed the mountainsides. This is to say that "invasions" of the haciendas, known in Colombia as the "colono problem," began on a large scale.

At first the government (the Conservative Party was in power) tried to cope with the situation by purchasing some of the large estates, dividing them into small parcels, and selling these small tracts to the campesinos. In all probability this merely whetted their appetites for more. In any case, in the government's efforts to obtain land some of the haciendas became involved in litigations in which it became abundantly evident that many of them were being held with no legal title whatsoever, others by means of deeds that were far from satisfactory, and still others by claims whose legality could not be established definitely. By 1926 some of these cases had reached the Supreme Court, and the stage had been set for one of the most momentous legal decisions in the history of the Colombian nation. That year the Court handed down a ruling to guide decisions in which there was a conflict between the claims of the State and those of an individual. In brief, the Court ruled that unless the professed owner could produce the original titles or deeds to demonstrate that the property had actually been alienated in a legal manner, the presumption was in favor of the claims of the State. The train of events set in motion by this decision is best described in the words of the man who was Director of the Departamento Nacional de Tierras at the time. In 1926 and subsequently he had to deal with the avalanche of conflicts over rights to the land which finally were responsible for the momentous Law 200 of 1936 which did so much to prepare the way for the national con-

---

[1] *Cf.* T. Lynn Smith, "Land Tenure and Soil Erosion in Colombia," in *Proceedings of the Inter-American Conference on Conservation of Renewable Natural Resources, Denver, Colorado, September 7-20,1948* (Washington, D. C., U. S. Department of State, 1948), pp. 155-160.

cern with agrarian reform that developed after democratic forms of government were re-established late in the 1950's. In one of his official reports this official, Dr. Guillermo Amaya Ramírez, had the following to say:

> The doctrine set forth by the honorable Supreme Court of Justice [. . .], despite its basis in elementary principles that are universally accepted, is producing as a tangible consequence an unbearable situation for the workers in the fields and one profoundly noxious for the national economy. In all parts of the Republic former arrendatarios [in Colombia an arrendatario is a worker who lives on the hacienda and who receives as a major part of his remuneration the use of a small plot of ground on which he erects his dwelling and grows a few subsistence crops] are suspending compliance with their obligations in the belief that the owners lack, as is true in many cases, the respective original titles: and persons from the outside are invading under the same pretext, not only the unused portions of the haciendas, but even the parts cultivated by those who figure as owners; so much so that the latter, fearful of appearing before the judicial power [. . .] initiate with the police of the respective *municipios*, who generally are on their side, actions which often amount to genuine ejections.[2]

In the midst of the confusion early in the 1930's the Liberal Party gained control of the national government and set about many reforms, including the enactment of the fundamental agrarian reform legislation embodied in Law 200 of 1936.[3] That legislation, by declaring that economic utilization was the fundamental basis for claiming rights to

---

[2] "Informe de Jefe del Departamento de Tierras y Aguas," *Memoria del Ministerio de Agricultura y Comercio*, Vol. II (Bogotá: Talleres Gráficos Mundo al Día, 1937), pp. 26-27.

[3] For some discussion of the background of Law 200 and a translation of parts of its text, see T. Lynn Smith, "Some Observations on Land Tenure in Colombia," *Foreign Agriculture*, XVI (1952), 119-123.

the land and by giving professed owners a period of ten years in which to demonstrate that they were making economic use of their holdings, eased the situation for some years. It may even have forestalled a violent revolution. Before the ultimate results could be determined, however, a period of chaos, violence and destruction, and virtual civil war had begun. Eventually, following the overthrow of the dictatorship and the establishment of a Government of National Union under Alberto Lleras Camargo as President, the interest in and development of an agrarian reform program became one of the principal preoccupations of Colombia's leaders. The studies and publications of some of Colombia's young intellectuals, who were called to head various ministries and bureaus, had much to do with this; in any case, by 1960 Colombia's endeavors had largely passed through the planning stage and entered one of action.[4]

INDICATORS OF THE NEED FOR AGRARIAN REFORM

The social and economic ills or the indicators which reveal the need for agrarian reform mentioned in these pages are those frequently encountered in the writings of various Latin Americans. To a considerable degree they correspond with those I have concluded are most significant, but the list that is given is by no means identical with the one that I would use if I were discussing agrarian reform in general. Some of those who read this volume would probably prefer to delete some of the items and substitute others that go unmentioned, and to this there would be no particular objection except in the case of some, such as latifundismo and the concentration of ownership and control of the land in general, which figure in almost every Latin American discussion of the need for agrarian reform. Moreover, it should be stressed that all of the items enumerated here are highly interrelated, since all are central features of essen-

---

4 For some of the studies most closely related to these developments, see Orlando Fals Borda, *Hombre y Tierra en Boyacá* (Bogotá: Editorial Antares, 1957); and Otto Morales Benítez, *Reforma Agraria: Colombia Campesina* (Bogotá: Imprenta Nacional, 1962).

tially the same social system. In all probability some of them are merely reflections of others in the list; nevertheless, they are thought to be adequate for purposes of the present diagnosis.

Latifundismo

In many parts of Latin America, and especially in such countries as Brazil, Colombia, and Venezuela, *latifundismo* has a special connotation which differs substantially from its meaning in other parts of the hemisphere. In these countries, only during recent years, and as the debate over agrarian reform waxed in volume and importance, has there been any tendency to designate as *latifundia* the highly developed plantations engaged in the production of sugar, coffee, rice, and so forth. Rather, the general rule has been to restrict the use of this term, presently so highly charged with opprobrium, to the extensive tracts of land that are either held in complete idleness or devoted to much less intensive uses than those for which they are eminently suited. As evidenced by the writings of A. P. Figueiredo slightly more than a century ago (of which extracts are given in Documents 1, 2, and 3), there has occasionally been a logical and eloquent plea for the imposition of a general property tax as a means of putting an end to the obvious disadvantages of these large unused or poorly used holdings, but until the recent imposition of taxes of 5 per mil by the state of São Paulo[5] in Brazil and 4 per mil in Colombia, such endeavors amounted to little more than voices crying in the wilderness. The powerful, landowning, upper-class families have seen to it that the right to levy a substantial tax on the land would not be invested in any governmental unit which they could not control. As a result land has gone untaxed, or practically untaxed, and the ownership of land has been in effect an asylum for capital. Economic pressures that would force the use of the soil have been lacking, and as Figueiredo indi-

---

[5] This measure was invalidated in 1963 by a constitutional change which terminated the right of Brazilian states to levy a general property tax, and, without any preparation whatsoever, gave this right to the municipios.

cated, agriculture has indeed been encircled by a barrier that could not be overcome by the man of modest means. In brief, in many parts of Latin America latifundismo per se, or the existence of millions of acres of fertile lands that are entirely unused, or utilized very poorly, in countries where the rural masses are unable to find land to cultivate and where the production of food and fiber is far below national needs, is a strong indicator of the need for agrarian reform.

High Degree of Concentration in the Ownership and Control of the Land

Merely because huge landed estates are not permitted to vegetate in idleness, so as to qualify them as latifundia in the Brazilian or Colombian sense of the term, does not mean that there is no need for agrarian reform in the areas in which large estates dominate the scene and determine the nature of the prevailing social system. As a matter of fact, if viewed from the standpoint of the world as a whole, a high degree of concentration in the ownership and control of the land is probably the most generally recognized indicator of the need for agrarian reform (exception being made, of course, for those countries in which experience runs a poor second to ideology and the huge state farm is idealized as a solution for their chronic agricultural problems). Certainly I would place this indicator first in importance, a conclusion, incidentally, which was reached on the basis of the sociological study of two sharply contrasting social systems in the United States some years before I was privileged to visit Brazil and other parts of Latin America. In one of these social systems which dominates rural life in the Midwest and many other parts of the United States, the family-sized farm is the central element in the complex; in the other, which is all important in many parts of the South and which also prevails to some extent in California and other western states, the large plantation is the nucleus of the social system which has generated so many of our nation's perennial social, economic, and political problems.

That there is a high degree of concentration in the ownership and control of the land throughout most of Latin America is made evident by practically every census of agriculture that is taken. In Brazil, for example, a country for which the data are among the best, the 1950 materials make it apparent that not more than one in four of the families that are dependent upon agriculture for a livelihood is headed by a person who could be classified as a farm operator. Moreover, even this proportion is inflated because the considerable number of squatters is included in the category of farm operators. This means that at least 75 per cent of Brazil's agriculturists fall into the unenviable category of farm laborers. Furthermore, of the minority that legitimately may be classified as farm operators (owners, renters, managers, and even squatters) almost 20 per cent have the use of no more than 13 acres, and 75 per cent have farms of less than 125 acres in size. Collectively this three fourths of all Brazilian farm operators have the use of only 10 per cent of the land in farms, whereas the 0.5 per cent of the operators with farms of more than 6,250 acres have more than 36 per cent, and the 0.1 per cent with estates of more than 25,000 acres have control of almost 20 per cent of the land in farms. Furthermore, between 1940 and 1950 the trend was in the direction of an increased concentration of the control of the land by the few.[6] It is true, of course, that the subdivision of land by inheritance is a powerful factor in fragmenting some of the holdings, but in Brazil its effects are apparently more than offset by those of other forces, and the need for agrarian reform becomes more acute as one decade is succeeded by another. In interpreting this information the reader should keep in mind that the Brazilian material represents the situation in a country that contains more than a third of the population and much more than a third of the area of all Latin America, and that the Brazilian data probably are fairly representative of what would be the case if the information for all twenty of the countries were available.

---

[6] For more details, see T. Lynn Smith, *Brazil: People and Institutions*, 3rd ed. (Baton Rouge: Louisiana State University Press, 1963), pp. 330-337.

High Proportion of Laborers in the Agricultural Population

The predominance of the large estate *ipso facto* means that a high proportion of the heads of all rural families are doomed for life to a position near the bottom of the social and economic scale. In Latin America, as elsewhere, unskilled workers inevitably have lower-class status, and of these the ones who are engaged in agriculture constitute huge segments of the lowest of the lowly. In addition, in many parts of Latin America large numbers of the agricultural laborers lead wandering, migratory lives; this residential instability makes their status and the social and economic roles they perforce must play much less enviable than they would be otherwise. Obviously, a high proportion of laborers in the agricultural population is merely a reflection of an extreme degree in the concentration of landownership and control, which was discussed above. Even so, the mere fact that three fourths of the heads of Brazilian families who live from agriculture are farm laborers, and the fact that the proportion in the remainder of Latin America is probably equally high, is a strong indicator of the need for agrarian reform. Until this proportion is substantially reduced one may confidently predict that it will be impossible either to increase the input of management in agricultural enterprises to effective levels, or to bring rural levels and standards of living up to the desired planes. Thus the need for agrarian reform shown by this indicator will continue until the vast majority of those who now gain a precarious livelihood through the sale of poorly executed and ineffectively applied labor, or their descendants, can either ascend the agricultural ladder and become farm operators or find remunerative employment in non-agricultural activities.

The Prevalence of Minifundia

In many parts of Latin America there is an acute need for agrarian reform even though high proportions of the agriculturists must be classified as farm operators, and even as owner-operators. This is true in extensive portions of such Andean countries as Venezuela, Colombia, and Ecuador where the mountainsides are blanketed with small, pocket-handkerchief-sized parcels of land, farms so small that they are utterly incapable of producing enough food and fiber to meet even the creature needs of those who live from agriculture. In a lesser degree a comparable phenomenon is present in many other countries. The existence of hundreds of thousands of minute, badly shaped, poorly tilled, and in-efficient farm units is only slightly less disadvantageous for those who live from the soil than a high concentration of ownership and control of the land. In a word, *minifundia* and *minifundismo* on a substantial scale is another of the indicators of the need for agrarian reform.

The statements above are founded for the most part on rather casual observation supplemented by the information from a few local surveys. As more adequate statistical data become available, though, these statements are found to be thoroughly justified. At the present time, for example, the materials from Colombia's first census of agriculture, taken in 1960, are beginning to appear. Unfortunately, the na-tional summary that has been published fails to present a tabulation showing the distribution of farms according to size. The report for the Departamento del Valle del Cauca, however, which was prepared under the direction of the man who was dean of the Faculty (or College) of Economics at the Universidad del Valle at the time of the enumera-tion, does give this all-important information in considera-ble detail.[7] It is quite unlikely that minifundismo in Colom-bia is most pronounced in the Departamento for which the data are available. Nevertheless, this enumeration indicated that of 50,171 farms in the Departamento, 25,957 (or 52 per cent) were plots of less than 5 hectares (about 13 acres) in area, and that 10,040 (or 10 per cent of all) of them were less than 1 hectare in size. Were the data tabu-lated properly for such Departmentos as Cundinamarca,

---

[7] *Cf.* Antonio J. Posada, organizer, *Censo Agropecuario del Valle del Cauca*, 1959 (Cali: Facultad de Ciencias Económicas, Univer-sidad del Valle, 1963), p. 11 *passim*.

Nariño, and Boyacá an even greater prevalence of minifundia would undoubtedly be revealed, and it is highly probable that if materials for all of Colombia were available the percentage of the farm operators having less than 5 hectares of land for their enterprises would exceed the 52 per cent registered for El Valle.

Brazil, of course, is not plagued by minifundia to the same degree as Colombia, Ecuador, and Venezuela. Nevertheless, as indicated by the 1950 data, one of five of her farm operators are utilizing tracts of land that contain less than 5 hectares; and it may be stated without fear of refutation that in many sections in South Brazil settled by peasants from Germany, Italy, Poland, and elsewhere in Europe, a continuous subdivision by inheritance of farms that originally were small is bringing the problem of the minifundia to an acute stage. There, as in southern Chile and in specific localities in all of the countries from Argentina to Mexico, small uneconomic farm units are indicative of a considerable need for agrarian reform.

Low Production per Worker

Although here and there one may find an exception, throughout nearly all of Latin America the production per worker engaged in agriculture is very low. This fact has been documented by so many economists and governmental officials that it seems unnecessary at this point to give any statistical demonstration of it. This low production per worker, in turn, is probably no more than a reflection of the effects of the socio-economic factors that are engendered and kept in force by a social system based on large estates, that is, by a high degree of concentration in the ownership and control of the land. Of all the factors involved, though, the following deserve specific mention: (1) the paucity of skills possessed and used by those who do the manual labor; (2) the extremely small input of management in the productive processes involved in Latin American agricultural and livestock enterprises (this deficiency is inevitable wherever the necessary capacities are not "built in" each person who participates in the tillage of the soil so that they may be applied day or night, any day or season of the year, to any particular square yard of soil, to any or all of the plants in any stage of their development, to every farm animal irrespective of where it may wander, and to every piece of farm equipment or machinery no matter to which part of the farm it may be taken); and (3) the lack of propulsions which will lead to regular work activities on the part of those who live from agriculture. All of these features are presently prominent parts of the systems of agriculture in vogue in most parts of Latin America. Indeed, in Brazil, Haiti, and the eighteen Spanish American countries taken as a whole at least one half of the agriculturists are dependent upon methods of extracting a living from the soil that are more primitive, less efficient, and more wasteful of human energy than those the Egyptians were using at the dawn of history.[8] The persistence of the complex of factors and forces which results in low productivity per worker, the inefficient combination of the factors of production, and the actual bemeaning of the rural population is eloquent testimony of the need for substantial agrarian reform.

Low Average Levels and Standards of Living

In the second half of the twentieth century man's knowledge of the earth on which he lives and of the ways of cooperating with nature in order to get products from the soil is sufficient to make possible a far greater abundance of goods and services than is presently being enjoyed by the people on most parts of the earth. In Latin America the aspirations of the people and the actual amounts of goods and services enjoyed are not as abysmally low as they are in some countries. Moreover, since the close of the Second World War, and, it should be emphasized, frequently in

---

[8] For a discussion of the nature of the cultural complex in action, which the present writer calls "the system of agriculture," and its role in social and economic progress, or the lack of it, see T. Lynn Smith, *The Sociology of Rural Life,* 3rd ed. (New York: Harper & Brothers, 1953), Chap. 14; and Smith, *Brazil,* Chap. 15.

quite unrealistic and sometimes in fantastic ways, the aspirations of the common people have risen spectacularly, whereas the rise in the actual level or plane of living has been in much more modest proportions. This has resulted in the broadening of the gap between the aspirations, or what properly is designated the standard of living, and the average amounts of goods and services consumed, or the level of living. In many places this gap has become so wide that it may reasonably be designated the "zone of exasperation." Probably this problem is not as great in the rural districts as it is in the urban centers of Latin America, but even in the agricultural and pastoral areas it is a problem that demands attention. Indeed, in most of the rural sections of Latin America the poorly directed aspirations of the masses and the prevailing low levels of living are indicative of the need for substantial modifications in the distribution of landownership and control, the systems of agriculture, the availability and functioning of educational institutions, the nature and vigor of local governmental institutions, and in various other aspects of a genuine agrarian reform.

Extreme Degrees of Social Stratification

Reference has been made above to the two-class system introduced into Latin America during colonial times and perpetuated there to a very considerable extent until the present time. In Latin American societies, as in others in which a system of large estates has dominated the social, economic, and political aspects of life, this has determined that there would be a small class of elite families at the apex of the social scale, and a large mass or class of impoverished, uneducated, unskilled, and only slightly productive workers at the base of it. Until late in the nineteenth century, when many thousands of peasant families were settled in southern Brazil, southern Chile, and parts of Argentina, Latin America's almost exclusively rural societies contained little or nothing in the way of middle-class farm families to help fill the broad void that existed between the upper and lower extremes of their two-class societies, that is between the small stratum of the elite and the huge masses of servile or semi-servile workers. If evaluated in terms of the standards which prevail widely in the world during the second half of the twentieth century, any society so constituted is certain to exhibit all of the indicators of the need for agrarian reform. Even if it were the only indicator available, however, such a system of social stratification would point strongly to the necessity for substantial changes in the institutional arrangements governing man's relations to the land.

This enumeration could be continued indefinitely, for wherever there is any considerable degree of concentration of the ownership and control of the land (even if this be in the hands of the state), low productivity, huge wastes of human potentialities, and a host of other social and economic ills are certain to abound. This is particularly true in areas such as Latin America in which the absence, or practical absence, of the general property tax enables land to become an asylum for capital and the problem of latifundismo to acquire sizable dimensions. The seven items included in this section, though, should serve present purposes of indicating that there is substantial need for agrarian reform in a great many parts of Latin America. It does seem desirable, however, to point out that this line of thinking is not merely that of the present writer, himself not a Latin American, by offering the diagnoses prepared by some of the Latin Americans themselves. Several of these are given in detail in substantial extracts from the writings of A. P. Figueiredo of Brazil (Documents 1, 2, and 3), Alfonso López of Colombia (Document 5), and José Flores Moncayo of Bolivia (Documents 10 and 11). To these may be added the list of indicators of the need for agrarian reform that was prepared in 1961 by the most noted writer in Brazil's lay Roman Catholic group. These are as follows:

1. A high proportion of illiterates and the consequent general lack of culture.
2. Poor sanitary conditions and high indexes of mortality.

3. Low agricultural production and overpopulation.
4. Low levels of marriage and family organization.
5. The absence of or an extremely low rate of technical progress.
6. The destruction of the soil, and, in general, the poor use of the land.
7. Defective distribution of landownership.
8. Serious smothering of the civic consciousness because of the debility of municipal [county] life, and more remotely through the general weakening of democratic life.
9. Lack of leadership.
10. A low degree of vertical social mobility and a high degree of geographical mobility.
11. Technical and legal deficiencies in the registration of titles to the land.[9]

THE OBJECTIVES OF AGRARIAN REFORM

There are extreme differences between the objectives of agrarian reform programs as these are proposed by Latin Americans of various social classes, philosophies and ideologies, professions, and nationalities. Many of the landless agricultural workers, whose cupidity is exploited by the revolutionaries, believe that agrarian reform means simply the confiscation of the large estates and their distribution in small plots among the workers. For them, and for the large masses of unskilled or semi-skilled workers in the cities, agrarian reform has essentially the same objectives as did the measures put into effect in Haiti during the French Revolution, the ideas widely disseminated among the ex-slaves in the southern part of the United States following the Civil War as expressed in the slogan "forty acres and a mule," or

---

[9] Gustavo Corção, "Conceituação da Reforma Agrária," (Mimeographed), presented to the Simpósio sôbre Reforma Agrária, organized by the Instituto Brasileiro de Ação Democrática, Rio de Janeiro, April 17-22, 1961. For a report of the proceedings of this symposium see José Arthur Rios, ed., *Recomendações sôbre Reforma Agrária* (Rio de Janeiro: Instituto Brasileiro de Ação Democrática, 1961).

the unfulfilled dreams of the peasants who supported the Russian Revolution. At the other extreme one encounters influential groups in Brazil, Chile, and some of the other countries, who will maintain that merely the "industrialization" or mechanization of agricultural production is all that is needed in order to designate the changes as an agrarian reform.[1]

Much more representative of the general thinking in most of the countries, however, are the "guide lines," or *diretrizes*, that were formulated early in the 1950's by the members of the National Commission on Agrarian Policy appointed by Brazilian President Getúlio Vargas with the then Minister of Agriculture, João Cleofas, as chairman. This Commission was established in compliance with the pledge of agrarian reform which Vargas had made in connection with his campaign for election. The members of this Commission formulated the document which is presented in full in translation on other pages of this volume (see Document 7), so at this point it is sufficient to call attention to the fundamental objectives of agrarian reform as agreed upon by the members of the group. The reader should note that they are two: (1) through the subdivision of latifundia and the grouping of minifundia, to provide an opportunity of becoming landowners to those who cultivate the soil; and (2) to valorize man and the land so as to ensure work and an honorable existence for all.

In 1952, but not until after the "guide lines" had been formulated, the present writer served as advisor to Brazil's National Commission on Agrarian Policy. At that time there seemed to be almost unanimous assent to the proposition that the primary objective of agrarian reform was the improvement in the quality and well-being of the average inhabitant of rural Brazil. This, in turn, involved the valorization of man, and, along with it, an improvement in the

---

[1] See, for example, the brochure entitled *Reforma Agrária Brasileira* issued in Rio de Janeiro in September, 1960, by the Conselho Superior das Classes Productoras. The conclusion of this little exposition, set forth in capital letters, is that "a Brazilian agrarian reform, therefore, is the industrialization of agriculture."

productive capacity of the land and the perfection of the institutions that govern man's relationships to the land. Perhaps it would be useful to indicate that the Brazilian term *to valorize* seems to mean the development of man's capacities in a way that would bring them somewhat nearer to his potentialities.

All of this had a familiar ring to one who had served during the period 1943-1945 as advisor to the Government of Colombia on matters pertaining to "colonización y parcelación" (or resettlement and the subdivision of large estates). This was an epoch in Colombia's history in which President Alfonso López and his brother Miguel López Pumarejo, who served as head of the Caja de Credito Agraria, were doing their utmost to develop a genuine category of middle-class farmers in Colombia. They had become convinced that Colombia would never enjoy anything resembling political stability until her agriculture was in the hands of capable, self-reliant, middle-class, owner-operator farmers such as they had observed in the Middle West and other parts of the United States and in various countries of western Europe. However, as Colombia's political history unfolded, that unfortunate nation was to undergo one of the most severe blood baths of modern times before much of the ground which they had prepared would begin to bear fruit. Even so, their concepts of the objectives of agrarian reform certainly had much to do with the present lines that this activity is taking in Colombia.[2]

Later on, in 1956, I drew on my experience in Colombia, Brazil, the other Latin American countries, and the principal agricultural regions of the United States, in the preparation of a lecture on agrarian reform which I presented in all of the principal cities in Brazil, from Belém to Rio de Janeiro, and in the Spanish American countries from Paraguay to Panama. At that time I indicated that the three principal objectives of agrarian reform are as follows:

---

[2] For a copy of the memorandum which the present writer prepared at the conclusion of his assignment in Colombia, see T. Lynn Smith, "Colonization and Settlement in Colombia," *Rural Sociology*, XII (1947), 130-139.

1. A genuine agrarian reform should effect substantial improvement in the abilities, capacities, and performances of those who cultivate the land to bring them more in line with human potentialities.

2. Any worth-while agrarian reform should result in a substantial increase in the amount of agricultural and livestock products secured from a given amount of land and the efforts of those who work it.

3. A real agrarian reform should result in the replacement of wasteful, inefficient, bemeaning, and stultifying ways of producing agricultural and livestock products by methods of agriculture that are efficient, dignifying, or ennobling to those engaged in agriculture and stockraising.[3]

Then, following a discussion of each of these propositions, I rephrased the basic objective of agrarian reform as that "of getting a nation's agricultural and stockraising activities highly concentrated in the hands of a middle social class of farmers." I cautioned, however, that before this basic objective could be attained it would be necessary to achieve the following lesser objectives:

1. The control of the land, as owners or as renters on long-term leases, must be placed in the hands of those who actually till it. This means the elimination, on the one hand, of any class of permanent agricultural laborers, by whatever name such workers may be called, and likewise the elimination of any privileges of a category of landlords through which they have virtual powers of life and death over the workers who toil on their estates.

2. Through education, training, and experience, the ordinary man who works the land must be developed

---

[3] T. Lynn Smith, "Reforma Agrária," *A Lavoura* (Rio de Janeiro), LIX (1956), 7-8; and T. Lynn Smith, *Current Social Trends and Problems in Latin America* (Gainesville: University of Florida Press, 1957), p. 34.

into a person who is capable of exercising with considerable facility the functions of the manager or entrepreneur and those of the capitalist or property owner, as well as those of the agricultural laborer. Each farmer must come to combine in his own personality all the attitudes, skills, and habits that go with the performance of the three basic economic functions of which the economist writes, namely that of the capitalist, that of the manager, and that of the laborer. In brief, this means teaching, encouraging, and enabling each future agriculturist to develop all of the qualities, skills, characteristics, attitudes, and habits of the middle-class farmer.[4]

Such objectives of agrarian reform are explicit or implicit in many of the extracts that have been translated and published in this volume, and they are also integral parts of the agrarian reform programs that are underway in such countries as Venezuela and Colombia. Moreover, they are basic thoughts of many of the proponents of agrarian reform in Central America, the Dominican Republic, Ecuador, Peru, Chile, Argentina, and Uruguay, as well as in Brazil. One of the more important Brazilian groups, following a week of intensive study and discussion, stated explicitly that "Agrarian reform is not essentially a change in the regime of property, although it cannot be accomplished without such a change." Rather, because it "seeks the creation of a rural middle class, an agrarian reform should place major emphasis upon a regime of properties distributed in accordance with this [middle-class] criterion." In general, "An agrarian reform of the democratic type is, then, a combination of political, cultural, and economic measures which should be employed where the indicators of a defective agrarian structure are observed to be the cause of subhuman conditions of life. This combination of measures should immediately bring about an elevation of the human level and the dignification of the rural populations; and it should also produce, as a consequence, an improvement in the general

---

[4] Smith, *Current Social Trends and Problems*, p. 37.

political, cultural, economic level of the population where it is applied." Finally, the group reached consensus on the proposition that "An agrarian reform of the democratic type, in a country such as [Brazil], although not consisting exclusively of an alteration in the laws governing rural property, cannot fail to provide a revision in those statutes that will alter the relationships between the agricultural classes and make it possible for larger numbers of persons to become landowners." [5]

Much the same conclusions were arrived at by Peru's Commission on Agrarian Reform and Housing. The exposition formulated by this group states categorically that:

> The agrarian reform may no longer be considered as the mere partitioning of the land or the readjustment of the rights of its proprietors. Its ends are much more elevated and complex. [. . . .].
>
> Agrarian reform, then, should be motivated in economic criteria and also in social criteria. To attend solely to the economic aspect will lead to the establishment or the maintenance of a purely materialist order, one lacking human sentiments. On the other hand, if too much emphasis is placed on social criteria, of a predominately distributive nature, the result will be not to overcome poverty but to make it more widespread.
>
> Any well-conceived reform, therefore, should seek to create and to maintain conditions which favor the sustained increase of agricultural production and the improvement of the position of agriculture relative to that of other productive activities, so as to secure a balanced development.
>
> Simultaneously, the reform should promote the equitable distribution of the agricultural income, facilitate access to the ownership of land by those who have the capacities to work it as independent farmers, create opportunities for education and the diffusion of culture,

---

[5] Rios, *op. cit.*, pp. 61-64.

and, in general, give stability to rural life, thus contributing to the integral progress of the nation.[6]

Finally, as mentioned above, the multiplication of family-sized farms and the improvement of the social and economic positions of the families owning and cultivating them are the major objectives of Colombia's agrarian reform program. Consider, in this connection, the following statement of objectives as given in her Agrarian Reform Law:

ARTICLE 1. Inspired by the principle of general welfare and by the necessity of extending to the ever-increasing sectors of Colombia's rural population the exercise of the natural right to property, harmonizing it with its conservation and use in the social interest, this Law has as its objective:

First. To reform the agrarian social structure through procedures designed to eliminate and prevent the inequitable concentration of property in land or its subdivision into uneconomic units; to reconstitute adequate units of cultivation in the zones of minifundia and to provide lands to those who lack them, with preference being given to those who will utilize them directly through the use of their own personal labor.

Second. To promote the adequate economic use of unused or deficiently used lands, by means of programs designed to secure their well-balanced distribution and rational utilization.

Third. To increase the total volume of agricultural and livestock products in harmony with the development of other sectors of the economy; to increase the productivity of the farms by the application of appropriate techniques; and to endeavor to have the lands used in the way that is best suited to their locations and characteristics.

Fourth. To create the conditions under which the small tenants and sharecroppers shall enjoy greater

---

[6] Comisión para la Reforma Agraria y la Vivienda, *La Reforma Agraria en el Peru: Exposición de Motivos y Projecto de Ley* (Lima: Talleres Gráficos P. L. Villaneuva S. A., 1960), pp. 28-29.

guarantees, and they as well as the wage hands shall have less difficult access to landownership.

Fifth. To elevate the level of living of the rural population, as a consequence of the measures already indicated and also through the coordination and promotion of services related to technical assistance, agricultural credit, housing, the organization of markets, health and social security, the storage and preservation of products, and the promotion of cooperatives.

Sixth. To ensure the conservation, defense, improvement, and adequate utilization of the natural resources.

In a later section of the Law (Chapter X, entitled *Unidades Agrícolas Familiares*, or Family-Sized Farms) some of these objectives were restated in even more concrete terms. Thus the first article in this Chapter reads as follows:

ARTICLE 50. In its colonization projects as well as in those involving the subdivision of estates and the concentration of small parcels, the Institute [the agency created to administer the program of agrarian reform] shall seek preferentially the creation of "family-sized farms."

By a family-sized farm is meant that which meets the following conditions:

(a) that the size of the tract, in accordance with the nature of the zone, the type of soils, waters, location, relief, and possible nature of the crops shall be sufficient, if utilized with a reasonable degree of efficiency, to provide to a normal family an income sufficient to cover its living expenses, to meet the payments on the purchase or improvement of the land, if this is involved, and to permit the progressive improvement of the dwelling, the farming equipment, and the general level of living;

(b) that the said extension normally shall not require for its use with reasonable efficiency more labor than that of the proprietor and his family. It is understood, though, that this last regulation is not incompatible with the employment of extra labor during certain periods of the agricultural work, if the nature of the farming operations makes it necessary, nor with mutual aid through which neighbors may help one another with specific tasks.[7]

METHODS OR TECHNIQUES OF AGRARIAN REFORM

Proposals for the accomplishment of agrarian reform programs in Latin America are of the utmost variety and there are even great differences among those that have figured in the reform measures attempted to date. Nor are the devices that will be used in the future likely to lack diversity and originality. In this respect, as in so many others, ways of organizing society's efforts that have been tried and tested in other parts of the world are not likely to gain preference over those which occur to the groups who succeed in getting control of the military and political power. Often the measures actually employed are likely to be mere improvizations, frequently with highly nationalistic colorations. Sometimes, as was the case in Bolivia, the legal measures will follow rather than precede the reform activities. Moreover, in most cases the major concern probably will be with the land and relatively little with the man who tills the soil and the institutional framework of the community within which he lives and works. This is to say that most programs for the distribution of landownership probably will not be accompanied by the necessary endeavors to educate and train those who farm the land nor by the organization of adequate facilities for transportation and communication, agricultural credit, marketing, technical assistance, health and sanitation, primary and secondary education, and so forth.

If those who are imbued with Russian, Chinese, or Castroist ideas are successful in seizing power in any of the

[7] Translated from the text of Ley 135 de 1961 sobre Reforma Social Agraria, as given in Otto Morales Benítez, *Reforma Agraria: Colombia Campesina* (Bogotá: Imprenta Nacional, 1962), pp. CDVII- CDXLV.

Latin American countries, there could even be much fanfare about an agrarian reform in which there was little or no distribution among the farmers of property rights to the land by the State, and the transformation, with a minimum of change, of the existing large estates into state farms or the so-called collective farms. Where the plantation system prevails, as in extensive portions of Latin America and also in such non-Latin parts of South America as British Guiana, such a transformation could easily take place with few or no sustained efforts to gain the support of the rural masses by promising them land of their own.

In the middle 1960's, however, it appears unlikely that Russian, Chinese, or Castroist models will be employed in the agrarian reforms in most of the Latin American countries. Ironically, though, the fact that the ways of organizing agricultural activities in the U.S.S.R., Communist China, and Castro's Cuba definitely do not bring forth an abundance of food and fiber seems to count for little in the present low esteem of the methods employed in the totalitarian countries. It is true that among some of the Latin American intellectuals there is an appreciation of the fact that in agriculture the only way of securing an adequate input of management is through the family-sized farm system, manned by middle-class farmers; but most Latin Americans are as oblivious to this fundamental point as are their fellows in Africa and other so-called underdeveloped parts of the earth. Be this as it may, the paths that are likely to be followed in agrarian reform endeavors in most parts of Latin America are liable to be neither the quick transformation of existing large estates into State or collective farms nor the relatively slow, unspectacular, and difficult work of developing a genuine system of family-sized farms operated by an able, independent, self-reliant, enterprising, and highly productive body of farmers of middle-class status. However, the patterns evolving in Colombia and Venezuela are indeed magnifying the family-sized farming elements in those countries. The same is true of the colonization activities in Uruguay and Argentina, which in effect have added substantial agricultural segments to the pastoral economies of those nations. Along with earlier colonization efforts in Argentina, Chile, and South Brazil, they are responsible for the major advances so far made in building along the lines that have produced such spectacular results in much of western Europe and in the United States and Canada.

The redistribution of property rights to the land is likely to prove the major element in the agrarian reform programs of almost all of the Latin American countries unless, perchance, they should develop along totalitarian lines, as now seems unlikely. Such a measure, though, requires specific ways and means by which the national governments regain the rights to the land that has been alienated, for it is not realistic to believe that adequate agrarian reform can be achieved merely by operations on the public domain as it now exists. Even in Brazil, Colombia, Bolivia, Venezuela, and the other countries in which huge portions of the nation's territory are still unsettled, genuine agrarian reform is largely a thing apart from the occupation of new lands. Therefore, highly important among the techniques of agrarian reform are the measures by which the state regains property rights to substantial portions of the arable and pasture lands within its limits. These measures, in turn, are of considerable variety.

Confiscation of landed properties is definitely one measure to be reckoned with. Following the successful struggles for independence from Spain, many of the Spanish American countries confiscated the estates of the Royalists and distributed them among the leaders of the revolts. More recently, in such countries as Venezuela and the Dominican Republic, the confiscation of the lands that members of the ruling families had gathered into their hands during decades of absolute power has provided broad expanses of the best land for use in agrarian reform programs. Confiscation on an even larger scale has characterized the programs in Cuba and Bolivia, where, as matters stand today, there seems to be no evidence of any substantial attempts to reimburse the former owners for the lands that were taken. Confiscation, thus, is a very real technique in Latin American agrarian reform programs. Indeed, because of the runaway inflation characteristic of the Brazilian economy, the demands made by the now former President Goulart for a constitutional change that would permit the government to take over private property (and this would have applied to all types of property and not merely to land) without reimbursement in cash was in effect a demand for confiscatory powers.

Expropriation of the land intended for subsequent distribution to the campesinos is undoubtedly the device most widely considered in connection with agrarian reform programs in Latin America. There is, however, little agreement with respect to the grounds upon which expropriation measures should be justified, the degree of reimbursement to be made, or the various other aspects of the subject. The Mexicans stress that their agrarian reform legislation prohibits the expropriation of land without immediate compensation, and similar regulations seem to prevail in most of the other countries. This, of course, does not mean that a revolutionary government may not suddenly come to power in one of them which would change these rules overnight. The declaration of Belo Horizonte, formulated by Francisco Julião and other Castro sympathizers in Brazil and apparently not objected to by a Brazilian president and prime minister, which is reproduced here in translation (Document 9), contains the formula of "repayment" in terms of long-term, low-interest, and non-negotiable bonds. Under the inflationary conditions which are chronic in Brazil and equally serious in several other countries, such a provision should probably be categorized as confiscation rather than expropriation. (Such runaway inflation, it may be said parenthetically, is an effective means for preventing the rise to ownership of the huge number of capable, industrious, and aspiring farmers who are presently hemmed in on a tenant status on Argentina's extensive *estancias*.)

If and when large-scale expropriation measures are put into effect, it is unlikely that remuneration will be made at the full cash or market value of the land; more likely either the value at which the land has been returned for tax purposes, or some multiple of that rate, will be enforced. In such actions Latin Americans are like their fellows elsewhere in feeling that those who have grossly understated the value of their property for tax purposes "get what they have coming" when such nominal values are the basis for reimbursement in expropriation cases.

The Mexican doctrine of "unaffectability" is also highly pertinent in connection with expropriation. Briefly, this has been applied to mean that certain portions of the estates, tracts selected by the owners themselves, are exempt from expropriation; and it appears that the same doctrine has been applied, perhaps illegally (or of doubtful legality), to extensive domains that were devoted to pastoral uses. As is apparent from a study of the extracts from the writings of Ramón Fernández y Fernández (Document 15) and Víctor Manzanilla Schaffer (Document 16), this "unaffectability" is one of the aspects of the Mexican agrarian reform in which change seems imminent. Under the best of circumstances such a provision would seem to open wide the gates for political favoritism and various other malpractices. As yet, however, it seems not to have been imitated elsewhere in Latin America.

As will be indicated below the need for expropriation would be greatly reduced, and perhaps eliminated almost altogether, if the various Latin American countries made substantial use of the general property tax, locally levied and spent, in order to get the funds needed for the support of essential services such as primary and secondary schools, health facilities, bridges and local roads, protection of life and property, and so forth. This is not the case, however, so instead of tax pressures which would force the economic use of the soil and provide the means whereby the local populations themselves could organize and secure many of the services and facilities they need so badly, local initiative is stymied. Indeed, the provision of educational and other services is tightly bound in a snarl of red tape that stretches from the community to the national capital, and debate

waxes hot over the social function of property rights to land
and the kind of laws needed to ensure that the owners will
put their land to some use.

The placing of ceilings on the amount of land is another
device that has been employed in many countries throughout the world in connection with agrarian reform programs.
In Latin America, though, comparatively little use has been
made of this particular measure as yet. The 500-acre limita-
tion provision in Puerto Rico is an excellent example of
such regulations, but neither Brazil nor any of the Spanish
American countries has put a similar law into effect. Perhaps the "unaffectability" feature of Mexican legislation is
the nearest thing to it so far attempted in any of them. The
placing of ceilings on the amounts of land that can be
owned by an individual, family, or corporation has the
effect, of course, of forcing the sale of some portions of a
large estate to the state or to other private owners.

Finally, it seems advisable to mention the acute need
for a public or semi-public agency that would be devoted exclusively to purchasing large estates at market prices when
they are for sale and reselling them in smaller amounts to
those with the necessary cash or credit who want to purchase
tracts of fertile and well-located land. There are numerous
reasons why such an agency is needed; the following are
among the principal ones: (1) many factors contribute to
the formation and perpetuation of large estates, and very
few to their subdivision; (2) throughout Latin America
many estates put together during colonial times persist to
this day, and many others have since been added to the list;
(3) these large estates include the most fertile and best-
located portions of the national territory; (4) the rich lands
which form parts of these estates are often used only for
grazing, and are often entirely idle, whereas agricultural activities are crowded onto the surrounding mountainsides or
other places poorly adapted for farming; (5) even if an
owner, or the one in charge of his estate after his death,
wishes to dispose of the property, the negotiations are almost always for the entire tract and not for a few hundred
acres of it; and (6) under these circumstances those with

sufficient money or credit to enable them to purchase and operate a family-sized farm are unable to find fertile and well-located land for sale in suitable amounts. Because the owner of a large plantation, hacienda, or *fazenda* can hardly be expected to go into the business of subdividing land, and because it is imperative that fertile acreage near centers of population and served by transportation facilities be made available in amounts suitable for family-sized farming operations, the agency mentioned above seems highly necessary. In this connection one may mention that by cooperative methods the Japanese colony of São Paulo, Brazil, has largely performed this service for itself. By 1958 the members of this group, a number that runs to many thousands, who began as agricultural laborers upon their arrival between 1934 and 1940, were nearly all owners of family-sized units in the state of São Paulo and, above all, in the area that lies within a radius of 40 miles of the city of São Paulo.[8] This example of the Brazilian Japanese indicates that, providing the human element is properly motivated and trained, the legal and other institutional patterns in Brazil make possible a rapid transition from large, poorly used or unused latifundia, to rich, productive family-sized farm units. At the same time it points to the need for measures that will enable other well-prepared and dynamic elements in the rural population, including the descendants of hundreds of thousands of Italians, Germans, and other Europeans, to purchase segments of existing large estates. One should not be too hopeful, though, that Brazilians or other Latin Americans will be enthusiastic about the establishment of any agency devoted merely to such prosaic purposes as the purchase, subdivision, and resale of farm land. Such an agency has also long been badly needed in the plantation and ranching districts of the United States.[9] However, even when the Federal Government was spending hundreds of

---

[8] *Cf.* Smith, *Brazil: People and Institutions,* pp. 315-317.

[9] *Cf.* T. Lynn Smith, *The Sociology of Rural Life* (New York: Harper & Brothers, 1940), p. 309, and the corresponding pages 322-323 in the second edition and page 323 in the third edition of the same book published in 1947 and 1953, respectively.

millions of dollars on "resettlement" programs, no such agency was established; nor has the Federal Land Bank System of the United States ever been willing to subdivide the large estates to which it has received title, even though many of its prospective customers were only interested in and in a position to finance family-sized farming tracts. Finally, neither the banks nor the insurance companies, with their tremendous holdings of agricultural real estate, have been willing to undertake the badly needed subdivision of large properties in the southern and western portions of our country. Actually, in view of our own inability to perceive the need for such an agency, those of us who live in the United States can hardly blame the Latin Americans if they are equally impervious in the matter. Thus the prospects are slight that any of the countries will actually establish an agency of the type mentioned. They are much more likely to expend all the money that they are able to secure for such purposes on colonization projects in which very high proportions of the total expenditures will be spent for planning and supervisory purposes and in which those in charge will prove to be totally unable to allow the farmers in the project to learn by the method of trial and error.

The crux of the matter of agrarian reform in Latin America, assuming that it will not involve making state and collective farms out of the estates presently held under private ownership, consists of ways and means of strengthening the position of those who are already the operators of family-sized farms and of greatly multiplying their number. The process by which responsible Latin Americans in substantial numbers have become convinced that the principal objective of agrarian reform is the development of middle-class operators of family-sized farms as the predominant features of the agricultural organization in their respective countries has not been quick and easy. The actual realization of such an objective is likely to prove even more difficult and time consuming. To date relatively few methods have been devised and employed in the attempt to attain this goal.

The first of these is the *promotion of immigration* of

farmers from other countries. During the last quarter of the nineteenth century this was used by the Brazilian government with considerable success in populating large segments of the three southernmost states of Brazil with small farming elements from Italy, Germany, Poland, and other portions of Europe; it was also used to some extent in Chile and Argentina. More recently such immigration has been promoted, mostly on a very small scale, as a part of various colonization ventures in Argentina, Brazil, Uruguay, and Venezuela. In Uruguay, where the colonists were allowed maximal freedom from interference by governmental functionaries, this program was responsible for the establishment of a substantial agricultural sector in the rural districts to complement the pastoral activities which long were the sole basis of the economy. In Argentina, too, immigrants established first in colonies contributed greatly to the development of agricultural activities, and others or their descendants now make up a substantial body of middle-class farmers, including owner-operators and the numerous renters presently stymied by rampant inflation on the tenant rung of the agricultural ladder. Other examples might be mentioned; but with the population of Latin America presently showing a natural increase of 3 per cent per year, immigration definitely is not the principal device to be employed in endeavors to get agricultural activities into the hands of a middle class of independent, self-reliant, and productive farm operators. Even in Brazil, the phenomenal success of the Japanese immigrants in the formation of a substantial middle-class farm element in the state of São Paulo, is hardly serving as a "pilot project" which other segments of the rural population are attempting to imitate.

The so-called *colonization projects*, or the establishment of closely supervised and directed groups of agriculturists on segments of what were formerly large estates, seem to be the principal device Latin Americans are employing in their endeavors to increase the number of family-sized farms and strengthen the position of middle-class farmers. Most of these endeavors suffer because, in the manner in which they are carried out, they are very costly. Under the best of circumstances the portion of the rural population which should be benefiting from agrarian reform measures that can be reached through colonization measures is very small. Moreover, it seems practically impossible to devise and supervise the projects in ways that will cause the managerial activities to become the responsibility of the farmers, rather than that of the supervisory personnel; and unless this can be done, most of the accomplishments of the projects are likely to be highly illusory. Thus, colonization is only a minor part of the answer to the basic problem of agrarian reform in Latin America. More general, less expensive, and more farmer-propelled measures are definitely needed.

In many countries much could be done merely by devising systematic ways of occupying the public domain, with features corresponding to the Jeffersonian system for surveying and giving titles to land, the encouragement of native populations and immigrants to participate in pushing forward the agricultural frontier, and the introduction of some kind of a homesteading procedure, such as proved so successful in the United States and Canada.[1] But, of course, although this could alleviate the situation in some of the already occupied portions of the respective countries and contribute greatly to the expansion of the economies, it would not obviate the need for substantial reform in the existing agricultural areas.

The pivotal measure in an integrated program of agrarian reform in most of the Latin American countries should be the imposition of a substantial general property tax. Such a tax should be levied and collected by the local governmental units and its proceeds used for the support of primary and secondary schools, the preservation of law and order and the protection of life and property, the provision of health and sanitary services, the construction and maintenance of local roads, and so forth. Nationally, in most cases, constitutional changes are required that would authorize the local governmental unit to place a tax upon the land and other real

[1] Cf. Smith, "Colonization and Settlement in Colombia," pp. 128-139; and T. Lynn Smith, *Sociología Rural* (Maracaibo: Universidad del Zulia, 1963), pp. 83-93, 124-125, and 131-132.

property; however, in each country, the central government should establish nation-wide minimal rates to be levied. Farms occupied and operated by their owners should be liable for a small established minimal amount, and then exempt up to a value of approximately 60 per cent of the assessed valuation of a well-equipped farm of adequate size to require the services of and provide the livelihood for the average middle-class farm family. Such a general property tax alone would be sufficient to sound the death knell for the latifundia, force the owners to put their land to work or dispose of it to someone who would, help terminate the general situation in which land is an asylum for capital, and greatly stimulate agricultural production.

In addition, a general property tax would institute a pooling of local resources to supply the funds (presently lacking and so badly needed), largely by self-help procedures and by getting contributions from all (including absentee owners), for the educational, health, law enforcement, and transportation services of the community. This, in turn, would be a long stride toward overcoming the prevailing debility of local government and the lethargy of local initiative. Likewise, through the schools and through the interchange of ideas between the farm operators, aided by agricultural extension services, it would set in motion forces that would eventually mean the replacement of primitive, labor-devouring, ineffective, inefficient, and stultifying agricultural methods by those that are efficient, productive, stimulating, dignifying, and socially esteemed. In a word, the imposition of a substantial tax on the land and other real estate could be the absolutely essential, initial step in a train of developments that would put the possession and use of the land into the hands of family-sized farmers, develop the capacities and abilities of those who work in agriculture so that they are much nearer human potentialities than they are at present, and provide the financial basis for genuine programs of community organization and development.[2]

---

[2] For some additional details of such proposals, see Smith, *Current Social Trends and Problems in Latin America*, pp. 38-44.

Two attempts have been made in recent years to make use of the general property tax as a part of agrarian reform programs in Latin America. One of these was the imposition by the State of São Paulo, Brazil, of a tax of 5 per mil upon rural real estate with the proceeds to be used for financing that state's program of *Revisão Agrária*. This was quickly checkmated, however, by Brazil's Congress which put through a constitutional change that stripped the states of power to levy a general property tax. The other is a general property tax of 4 per mil levied by the national government in Colombia with the provisions that the funds are to remain in the municipios (or counties) and to be used for educational and other features of community development programs.

In conclusion, it seems necessary to stress that most agrarian reform proposals and programs in Latin America are lacking in adequate measures for bringing about the needed changes in the human factor and the necessary modifications in the small local world, the society in miniature, or the community in which the lives of individuals and the activities of families are engulfed. Nevertheless, without primary consideration to the ways and means of developing qualified operators of family-sized farms and for establishing the necessary institutions and services at the community level, mere programs for redistributing the rights to the land are likely to prove illusory. Individually, most of the agricultural laborers may be benefited to some extent, but for the other segments of the rural population and for society as a whole, such incomplete measures are likely to prove disappointing if not entirely disastrous.

PART I

The Development of Concern about Agrarian Reform in Latin America

Introductory Note

For the most part, treatises dealing with agrarian reform
have followed rather than preceded reform projects and activities throughout Latin America. Nevertheless, some nota-
ble expositions appeared in some of the countries long before any substantial reform measures were attempted in
them, and others came into being in the course of the efforts
to correct some of the chronic ills in the institutions that
govern man's relationship to the land. In this section are presented translations of extracts from five expositions which
are unexcelled for the light they throw upon the background of agrarian reform in Latin America.

Three of these, all succinct, are from the writings of A. P.
Figueiredo of Recife, Pernambuco, Brazil. This man's
analyses and proposals were fully 100 years ahead of his
time, and they dealt with the situation in northeastern
Brazil, which continues to be the greatest problem area in
Brazil and possibly in all Latin America. The extracts selected for translation deal with the need for agrarian reform, the objectives of agrarian reform, and techniques of
agrarian reform, respectively.

The other two extracts, both somewhat longer than the
selections mentioned above, are from the pens of outstanding Colombians. One of these, the observant and lucid Salvador Camacho Roldán, saw and described the family-sized
farming sections of the midwestern United States as they
were during the 1880's. The second comes from one of the
addresses of Alfonso López, who was President of Colom-

bia during the 1930's. It indicates in no uncertain terms why his government felt compelled to attempt agrarian reform measures.

THE NEED FOR AGRARIAN
REFORM IN BRAZIL (1847)
A. P. Figueiredo

In our coastal plains, in the areas about our great population centers, there are vast expanses of land, most of it fertile, of which only a tenth, and frequently a hundredth, is cultivated. In these lands internal colonization should be put into effect. They should be put at the disposition of the workers. But these areas were alienated many years ago; they are in the possession of legitimate owners, and their location with respect to commercial facilities for exportation gives them a high market value. The government is far from being able to buy them. Therefore, it is necessary to take recourse to some other means. What is this means? That which is indicated to us, in a very evident manner, by a quick survey of the way in which the turbulent class of our population was formed, of which we have spoken, and which, impelled by necessity, becomes the effective cause of our other policies and even of our many other ills.

Among us, as among all other young countries, the popu-

Translated from A. P. Figueiredo, "Colonisação do Brasil," *O Progresso* (Recife), II (1847), 632-637.

lation goes on increasing and the fecundity of unions is fantastic, in cities and towns as well as in the country, and above all in the large cities such as the one in which we live. Let us examine what comes from this increase of population, first here in Recife and then in the interior. We shall not speak of the rich families because they are few and, furthermore, they are becoming impoverished generation after generation through the subdivision of property by inheritance; instead we are concerned with those in moderate circumstances and the poor. The daughters overburden these families, creating for them new necessities which in commerce result in many bankruptcies and also give rise to an insatiable thirst for public employment; among the poor this leads to results still more deplorable for public morals. The boys, if the parents have the means, go to school and then seek employment; if the parents are poor, they learn a trade and in this manner increase the number, already excessive, of tailors, shoemakers, masons, carpenters, etc., and bring about a ruinous competition among themselves, and often they are without work. Some go to establish themselves in the interior, but in small numbers. Because of this, we ask what destiny has the continued increase of population in the interior? Will they come to be employed in agriculture? No! The best elements will come here to Recife to seek their fortunes, to solicit a ridiculous employment; and the remainder will move to the towns and other population centers to pass lives of misery because we have no industry to offer steady work and regular pay to the free worker.

This is the source of those masses of men who lack secure means of existence and who in certain spheres feed the politics of the parties and in the lower strata of society practice robbery in all its varieties.

Why is it that the offspring of the families of some means, instead of entering the precarious paths of public employment, do not engage in commercial activities, or, what would be even better, why do they not engage in agriculture? Why, instead of learning to be tailors, masons, and carpenters, do not the sons of families slightly favored by fortune return to the interior; and why do they not become agriculturists? Why, unless forced to do so, do not the inhabitants of the forested zones cultivate the soil? Why do their children seek out the towns? For all of these questions there is only one answer, and unfortunately it is fully complete.

In the social state in which we live, the means of subsistence of the father of a family do not increase in proportion to the number of his children, with the result that in general the children are poorer than their parents and possess less capital. At present agriculture and commerce, and especially agriculture, are encircled by a barrier that cannot be surmounted by the man of slight means, for all of those who do not possess a considerable amount of wealth [. . .]. Agriculture, the productive function par excellence, the mother (alma mater) of nations, is where the vital interests of our country reside; and since it is encircled by a barrier, it is necessary that this barrier be torn down, let it cost what it may.

And what is this barrier? It is the large landed estate. This terrible entity has ruined and depopulated Ireland, the plains of Rome, and many other countries.

The culture in which our population should be occupied and which one day will give us a middle class and establish the validity of our representative system, as we have already demonstrated, is not that on a large scale, which demands large amounts of capital, and which here is carried on by slaves; it is culture on a small scale, which can be performed by the father of a family and his sons, aided at the most by a few hired workers during the periods of planting and harvest. But the lands which are most advantageous for small-scale farming, because of the nature of the soil, the availability of springs and creeks, and the nearness to centers of consumption and exportation, are not those of far-distant *sertões*, nor those of the rolling, sunburned plains (*catingas*) which have been reduced almost to sterility by the imprudent activities of the cotton planters. The lands [most suited for family-sized farms] are those near the sea-coast; in our provinces they are in the region occupied by the *engenhos* [sugar-cane plantations]. This region, which extends along the entire coast of our province and to a depth of 10, 12, and even 15 and 18 leagues, is, as is well known, divided into plantations or estates whose dimensions vary from one fourth of a square league to 2, 3, and even 4 or 5 square leagues. Here, because the culture of the sugar cane requires a special type of soil which is not found in all parts of the area, it follows that in addition to the cane fields, the necessary woods and the lands needed for the cattle and for the fields of mandioca, indispensable for the feeding of the slaves, the majority of the engenhos contain huge extensions of unused lands, lands that would be eminently suited for small farming, and which, if they were cultivated, would suffice to supply an abundance of mandioca flour, beans, and corn for the entire population of the province, for the neighboring provinces, and even for export.

But the owners refuse to sell these lands, or even to rent them. If one is wealthy, then he can buy an engenho; but if his means are slight and he wishes to buy or rent a few acres of land, he will not find them! This is what creates the unproductive population of the cities, the class of those seeking public employment, which increases daily. This is what causes the crimes against property to become more frequent and what daily impoverishes the country, since the number of consumers is growing, whereas that of the producers either remains constant or at least increases more slowly. But, say the large landowners, we are far from refusing poor people the land they need to cultivate; let them come and for a modest charge, or even gratis, we will give them not merely land to plant but also timber with which to construct their homes. This is true, but these favors which you landowners bestow upon them only continue at your pleasure. At any moment you may, either because of your own capriciousness or because they refuse to vote for your candidates in an election or because they fail to carry out any order you may give them, eject them without recourse. How can you ask them to plant, if they have no certainty of being able to harvest? What incentive is there in this for them to improve the land from which they may be expelled at any moment? On your lands they enjoy no political rights, because their opinions must perforce be in accord with your own; for them you are the police, the courts, the administration—in a word, everything; and, except for the right and the possibility of leaving you, these unhappy beings are in no way different from the serfs of the Middle Ages.

The power of the great landowners of the interior (and this power is great) is based upon the number of these obedient vassals that they maintain on their estates. Thus, because of the weakness of the government in comparison with these powerful individuals, it is impossible for a respect for the law to be extended to the interior. Under these circumstances each proprietor is obliged, as best he can, to maintain a kind of private militia so as to avoid being tyrannized by his neighbors or political adversaries, transformed into police authorities. In order that he can dispense with part of his lands, and consequently with a part of the influence of his armed forces, it is neccessary for his neighbors to do the same and for the government to become sufficiently strong that it can protect all of them against possible aggressions.

But there is only one effective means for obtaining a result of this kind: to restrain all of them, simultaneously, by an external force; and we find this force in the direct taxation which is authorized in our Constitution and in the general property tax which we have already proposed in other pages of this periodical and the advantages of which we have already demonstrated. If it were gradually extended throughout the province this land tax would force the large landowners to get rid of the lands which are of no use to them. These lands, subdivided among numerous individuals, would be the source of a middle class of small farmers who would augment the production of the nation on a large scale and contribute greatly to the government with respect to the maintenance of public order. Then, with all of its sons occupied productively and advantageously, Brazil could issue a call for the excess of the industrious populations of Europe to whom it could offer work and secure means of existence. Other than this, any attempts at colonization are absurd.

2

THE OBJECTIVES OF
AGRARIAN REFORM
IN BRAZIL (1846)
A. P. Figueiredo

❧

Here we shall be concerned only with the measures that should be taken to replace with a regular government the despotic oligarchy that oppresses us. This despotism, here in our land of Pernambuco, is no exotic fruit; it was not invented by the Cavalcanti family, nor by the presidents that have succeeded one another since the date of our independence. Nor does it come from the greater or lesser degree of morality in the government; it results logically and inevitably from the fact that the political form of the government is not in harmony with the state of social organization, with the actual distribution of wealth and of the instruments of production.

The nature of a constitutional government consists in giving the individual security against the possible despotism of the social authority, which is always supposed to be very much more powerful than the separate individuals who make up the nation; this is the case in Europe where the

Translated from A. P. Figueiredo, "Pernambuco in Retrospect (1846)," *O Progresso* (Recife), I (1846), 297-299.

authority has the support, to aid it in the administration of the laws, of the disinterested mass of citizens.

But with us, the authority and the individuals are in totally different circumstances. The major part of the land in our province is divided into great estates, remains of the ancient *sesmarias* of which very few have been subdivided. The proprietor or the renter occupies a part of them and abandons, for a small payment, the right to live on and cultivate the other portions to 100, 200, and sometimes up to 400 families of free mulattoes or blacks, of whom he becomes the protector but from whom he demands absolute obedience and over whom he exercises the most complete despotism. As a result of this the guarantees of the law are not for these unfortunates, who make up the large majority of the population of the province, but are for the landowners of whom three or four, united by ties of blood, friendship, or ambition, are sufficient to obliterate, in vast expanses of territory, the power and influence of the government. Thus these modern feudal barons, when their estates are located far from the provincial capital, live in an almost complete independence, administering justice with their own hands, arming their vassals for open warfare with one another, in disobedience to the orders of the government and the decrees of the judges: this is what goes on in the interior of the province. For such a state of affairs there are only two effective remedies: the first is a return to the old forms of absolute government, which invests the central power with extraordinary control; the second is to create immediately, at the expense of current feudalism, a middle class which will permit the constitutional government to proceed normally, in the interest of all, supported by public opinion and by material force that is independent of individual intrigues and much greater than the opposing coalitions of personal interests.

Now the first of these alternatives is nothing but a step backward; and we would never recommend, in order to correct a temporary problem, the restoration of these ancient obstacles, whose destruction has cost rivers of blood of all civilized peoples. Therefore, it is necessary to resort to the second alternative, which is the creation of a middle class. Now there are only three sources from which a middle class may be derived: commerce, industry, and agriculture. At present commerce actually occupies and makes unproductive a much larger number of individuals than are needed for the exchange of our products. Large-scale industry, in a country as poor as ours in capital and scientific knowledge, and where the interest rate is so high, can only be created by placing a terribly high tax upon the consumers; as for small industry, it is already overburdened and complains of the competition. Hence, only agriculture remains. Now in order that agriculture may make possible the rapid creation of a middle class it is essential that people of slight means be able to obtain lands and cultivate them with the certainty of enjoying the products. These conditions do not exist today, because the owners of sugar-cane plantations or the *fazendas* obstinately refuse to sell any portion of their lands, source and guarantee of their feudal power, and because the unfortunate occupant who takes the risk of planting remains at the mercy of the proprietor, who may expel him from the land within twenty-four hours.

3

TECHNIQUES OF
AGRARIAN REFORM
A. P. Figueiredo

How does it happen that with us agriculture is out of reach of all those who do not possess considerable wealth? All of you know, gentlemen, that it comes from the manner in which our land is subdivided; it is the necessary result of the large landed estate. The same effects that the celebrated economist Sismondi de Sismondi identified in the Roman countryside, and in unfortunate Ireland, we see reproduced here today, on a lesser scale with respect to the feeding of the masses because of the vast extension of our territory, but on a larger scale in its political aspects, because of the relative weakness of the government.

You know, gentlemen, that our province is divided naturally into three regions. The first is occupied in sugar making, and it extends from the seashore for 15 or 20 leagues to the interior. The second extends to the upper limits of the basins of the Capibaribe, the Ipojuca, and the Una. Fi-

Translated from a political speech by A. P. Figueiredo, reported in *Lidador* no. 205 of August 16, 1847, and reprinted in *O Progresso* (Recife), II (1847), 674-677.

nally, the third includes the affluents of the São Francisco. The absolute lack of roads places the latter region entirely outside the movement of production and exportation of the province. The central region, ruined by the destruction of the forests, and by the droughts produced by it, cannot be counted upon for a fixed production and, in addition to this, it is far from Recife, our center of consumption and exchange. There remains, then, the region of the littoral, in which is concentrated three fourths of the population of the province; it is the only one capable, under present conditions, of producing in abundance and of finding buyers for its products. But this region, except for some sandy, unhealthful stretches along the coast which are unsuited for most crops, is divided into great landed estates, fragments of the ancient *sesmarias* [huge land grants].

From the Abiay River to the Persenunga River, if you lack the means to buy or rent a sugar-cane plantation or other huge property, you will not find an inch of cultivatable land to buy or rent; even so, nine tenths of the land in the area is unused. They will offer lands for you to cultivate, but without any guarantee whatsoever, reserving to themselves the right to expel you any day that it suits their pleasure. Wherever man has no assurance of enjoying the fruits of his labor, he will not work; for this reason, the occupant of the sugar-cane plantation plants hardly anything in the clearing surrounding his hut, and, fearful each moment of being ejected, lives by transporting the sugar cane of the landowners. Thus, instead of the countryside offering a place for the excess population of the cities and towns, quite to the contrary, it is adding to the excess of all those who seek to get away from such a precarious and dependent mode of life. Whose fault is this, gentlemen? Is it that of the large landowners? No; they are obeying the law of necessity. The obedient vassals, who, under the name of *moradores*, are maintained on his lands by each of the large landowners, are needed by the latter to defend themselves against usurpations and aggressions, from which the Government is much too weak to protect them.

There is in this, gentlemen, on a small scale, something

analogous to the question of general disarmament that is agitating Europe. In order for one nation to be able to diminish its power to make war it is necessary that all the others do likewise; here, in order for one *senhor de engenho* to be able, without placing himself in danger, to sell or rent a part of his lands and in this way diminish the number of his vassals, it is necessary that his neighbors do the same. Because of this, gentlemen, it is essential that all of them simultaneously be exposed to a superior force. This force, gentlemen, is not to be found except in the direct imposition, promised by our Constitution, of the tax upon land. The establishment of this tax in proportion to the area possessed, and if necessary making it weigh more heavily upon unused lands than upon those that are cultivated, will force the large landowners to sell or lease those immense tracts of fertile lands which today are lost to agriculture and give work to only a small number of hands; then (or at least so I believe) not only will we be able to employ all of our people usefully, but also to invite the industrious populations of Europe, a thing which today would be gross insanity.

I understand, gentlemen, that many years will be required to extend the land tax over the immense area of our province. But even these delays are necessary and useful. The twenty or thirty years that must pass before it is possible to terminate the scientific work needed in order to extend this impost to our most remote areas will be advantageous; it will allow time for the construction of the roads that are needed to put the provinces in easy communication with the coast; and it will avoid the flagrant injustice of imposing the same burden upon the lands in the coastal districts, which are the areas of export crops and for this reason have a high value, and upon those in the interior which, for the lack of means of communication, attract very few buyers.

Gentlemen, the party of the opposition promises you that it will make use of all its power to put into effect this land tax which the Constitution promises us, and which today falls within the jurisdiction of our provincial assembly. These doors of agriculture and commerce, today closed to our fellow citizens, shutting them out from benefits of fortune, it promises you will be opened; and in this endeavor it counts upon your unanimous support.

Time is too short, gentlemen, to demonstrate to you how rich in beneficial results such a measure will be for our province. But the great landowners will have no more vassals, and the present moradores will be transformed into thousands of small landowners who will sustain public order and be a guarantee against the despotism of the authorities. Production will double; justice will be extended without difficulty to all parts; and elections, which today in the interior are merely a parody upon the constitutional system, will change their character and will shortly come to represent the opinion of the country.

This done, gentlemen, that which is legitimate in the popular hatred of the oligarchy and of foreigners will be satisfied without any disruption of justice and with great advantages for our country. Commerce and agriculture, today closed to our poor compatriots, will be opened to them. Our population will find abundant means of existence and we will not be forced to say, as we are today, that Brazil is overpopulated.

4

EARLY RECOGNITION
OF A MODEL FOR
AGRARIAN REFORM
Salvador Camacho Roldán

❧

Among the causes of the prosperity of Anglo-Saxon America I consider the principal one to be the system adopted from the beginning for the distribution of the public lands in small allotments, which put within reach of the worker this primary element of all riches, the first condition of independence and of personal dignity among men, and the indispensable basis of political equality, without which republican forms are a fraud. This system and the institution of the Homestead Law, which established the cultivation of the land by the worker as the only way of acquiring the ownership of land and which assured its possession by the family, has given an enormous stimulus to labor to the proletarian classes; it has completely changed the conditions of the ancient social organization, which placed the land in the hands of a few privileged persons; it has established imperishable bases for democracy; it has founded upon general participation the most perfect cooperation between those involved; it

Translated from Salvador Camacho Roldán, *Notas de Viaje* (Bogotá: Librería Colombiana, 1897), pp. 677-683.

has cheapened the price of the means of subsistence; it has been a powerful attraction to immigrants from other countries; it has given the incentive for the construction of a vast net of railways; it has sustained the demand for domestically manufactured goods; and it has created in all parts new articles for international trade.

Indeed, what, if not the hunger to acquire the ownership of land, has attracted this enormous current of American and European migrants to populate the solitudes of the West and to found these new and powerful States in the Valley of the Mississippi? What, if not the demand created by the extremely numerous and well-to-do *farmers* of these new regions, supports and sustains New England's mills for manufacturing textiles of cotton and wool, machinery, and agricultural implements? Who, if not these four or five million small owners, collect in their harvests these hundreds of millions of loads of corn and wheat and fatten each year these forty million hogs, and care for and milk these sixteen million milk cows, the products that make up two thirds of the food of the American people and two thirds of the articles exported? And where, if not in the Mississippi Valley, among these virile cultivators of the soil, were first organized the hundreds of regiments of volunteers who, under the command of Grant, Sherman, Sheridan, and Thomas, gave the stroke of death to the slave-holding Confederacy at Mill Springs, Fort Donaldson, Vicksburg, Pittsburg Landing, Chattanooga, and Nashville? Is not the aspiration to become owner of a small piece of land, to become free of the *rack-rent*, of the ever-increasing rent of the already monopolized lands of Europe, the principal thing which leads English, Irish, and German cultivators to abandon their homes in numbers of more than half a million per year in search of security and dignity in the American prairies? Is not the competition of millions of those who sell the foodstuffs that which, by lowering the prices of these, makes life easy, cheap, and abundant in these regions?

The large mass of owners of small farms, established principally in the West, today dominates the elections in this Republic and maintains the equilibrium between the semi-feudal ideas of the large proprietors of the South, the aristocratic tastes of the wealthy owners of the factories in New England, and the magnates of speculation in the central States of New York, Pennsylvania, and New Jersey. The presidency of the Union was, for forty-four years, the patrimony of the South, with Washington, Jefferson, Madison, Monroe, Jackson, and Tyler; it passed then to the dominion of New York and Pennsylvania, with Van Buren, Fillmore, and Buchanan; for thirty years now it is the West that has elected Lincoln, Grant, Hayes, Garfield, and Harrison, coming from the States of Illinois, Ohio, and Indiana: Lincoln and Garfield, woodcutters in their youth; Grant, a worker in hides; and Harrison, grandson of another President, prematurely deceased, who in his early years was also a backwoods farmer and resident of a log cabin.

Thus, it is in the United States that one can best study the change that the nineteenth century is beginning to bring about in the conditions of the collective life of the people. The ancient world was the kingdom of privilege, of the shameful exploitation of the multitudes in favor of the few, of the luxury of the aristocrats amidst the destitution and misery of the masses. In the French Revolution there arose, alongside the nobility and the clergy, the Third Estate, into whose composition entered the manufacturers, the merchants, those in the liberal professions, and the scholars and writers: at the present time the Fourth Estate is already surging forward in the form of the body of artisans and laborers who have received the right to vote in elections. In the United States, in 1880, of nine million of those who cultivated the soil, nearly five million were landowners and barely four million were agricultural wage hands. In this shines forth, therefore, the aurora of the redemption of the oppressed. Those who were previously slaves hitched to the ball and chain, later serfs of the glebe, and still later sharecroppers, have already begun to be the owners of the land which they water with the sweat of their brows. And this transformation is not as a result of the blood of martyrs, nor by means of a violent convulsion of the social structure with a promise of order and peace, but through the slow and sure action, peaceful but victorious, of the best type of human social organization.

Of all the grandeurs that I had the opportunity to see during my rapid trip through the heart of that country, none appeared to me so great as this social fact, because the independence, the liberty, and the equality of men does not consist in mere words written as a promise in the political constitutions, but in true and tangible facts which place men on the road to redemption. How can anyone consider as a *free man* the one who for his subsistence and that of his family is dependent upon the will of a landlord? Can there ever be equality between a wage hand and his patron? More fearful than the tyranny of men is the tyranny of things, and this result of the functioning of an institution suffices for the understanding of the difference which should exist between peoples who have their historical point of departure in the feudal control of the land and those who have sought to establish themselves by means of an equitable distribution of this primary basis of production in proportion to its occupants' capacity to work.

I do not ignore the fact that this subject constitutes one of the great scientific questions that divide modern economists in the evaluation of the respective merits of the known forms of individual property rights to the land: the ownership of large tracts of 500 or more hectares, the medium-sized property of from 20 to 500 hectares, and the small parcels measuring from a quarter of a hectare to 20 hectares. I am not unaware that the large property—if cultivated by its owner, which rarely is the actual case—facilitates the investment of large amounts of capital in improvements such as irrigation, drainage, the use of costly machinery, and the division of labor, which are beyond the reach of those of modest means who are dedicated to the cultivation of small acreages. Nevertheless, I also know that the medium-sized property can secure all of these facilities by means of association and cooperation. Every day these means receive new practical applications, one of which is the central factories for the processing of milk products in the United States, and the execution of certain agricultural tasks, such as the plowing of fields and the cutting and threshing of wheat, by contractors who deal with the farmers, who make use of the steam plow and perfected harvesting and threshing machines. Be as it may the result of these discussions, if the large property can be more or less defended from the economic point of view, it cannot be from the social point of view, that is, from that of the inequality of conditions of men, the most fecund source of perversion, injustice, and evil passions in human societies.

Moreover, one cannot deny that the concentration of the ownership of the land in a few hands is an instrument for concentrating wealth among the smallest number of producers; this leads to the development of luxury, of artificial pleasures, and of vices among the few and the degradation of the others, all of which results in the creation of useless riches, since they are not employed in the satisfaction of true necessities. As between better production and better distribution of the riches, the moralist and even the economist always favor the latter. For my own part, in summary, I believe the principal problem of modern societies consists in seeking, through natural means, the elimination of unjust institutions and better distribution among the producers of the values created by production.

5

LATIFUNDISMO AND THE NEED FOR AGRARIAN REFORM IN COLOMBIA

Alfonso López

﷽

There is deception, the product of deliberately misleading information about official objectives, when the attempt is made to create the opinion that the government is an enemy of the rural proprietor who, through his efforts, has succeeded in establishing enormous *haciendas* within which the greater part of the area is developed and in permanent production. In dealing with these landowners the government does not intend to follow any other policy than that of ensuring favorable and humanitarian conditions for the working class—day laborers, *arrendatarios*, and peons—and of preventing the continuance of certain feudal forms in the labor contracts and in the relationships between the owners of the land and the workers. When one recalls that there are still regions in Colombia in which the *campesino*, day la-

From a Message by President Alfonso López to the Congress of Colombia, July 24, 1935. Translated from the reproduction given in Marco A. Martínez E., *Régimen de Tierras en Colombia* (Bogotá: Talleres Gráficos Mundo al Día, 1939), Vol. I, pp. 16-17.

borer, or arrendatario not only lacks guarantees and security in his work but must endure systems of punishment and contributions imposed by individuals against the provisions of our laws, he doubts greatly that there has yet come to us that Christian and democratic civilization which has cost the world so many bloody revolutions and wars, and whose principles were the motive and the banner of the liberation of the New World.

The security of the hired laborer should be of no less concern to the State than security for private property, because both are social functions which cannot be left with excessive liberty, without the risk that they will be caught up in anarchical movements, in the shocks between antagonistic forces which are struggling for an equilibrium. If the agricultural proprietors and operators find it advantageous to be governed merely by the law of supply and demand in the labor market, being free to employ cheap hands and dismiss the more costly ones, they must accept the consequences of this mechanical economy with all its excesses. The miserable, uprooted, wandering masses who go about from one place to another in search of work, without finding it amid favorable conditions, will always be disposed to listen to the voices of the agitators who play upon their instinctive desires for usurpation and awaken them to the unjust contrast between their economic situation and that of the landowners. The campesino seeks stability, not revolution. He aspires to have a plot of ground of his own, where he can rear a family without fear of returning to vagabondage and misery. The proprietor can give it and he does so in the majority of cases; but the landowner cannot resign himself to being deprived of the feudal and supreme right of ridding himself of the worker, of ruining him if it is profitable, of razing the results of years of toil, even though he may have to pay for it. The irritation and bad state of affairs which recently were produced on some large coffee plantations were born of similar causes. Before the eyes of the workers whom the master had dismissed, the huts that had been erected under such difficulties by the arrendatarios and their families were burned, without the excessive cruelty of this act of dispossession being mitigated by a payment for the improvements. The campesino saw in this an exhibition of the inhuman and uneconomical action of the rich, protected by judges and officers, against the poor. Crops and huts reduced to ashes, purchased at any price merely to be burned, are crimes against the Christian concept of the land, which venerates work ennobled by religion as a way to moral perfection. And these crimes are being committed. In this way private property is being defended from the aspirations of the laborer also to become a proprietor; in this way a wall of hate is being raised between those who perforce must be collaborators in a common enterprise; in this way the function of property ownership is being held up to labor as its antagonist and rival.

Many property owners, upon observing the agitation— often justified, sometimes unjustified but explicable—solicit from the State the forces for maintaining public order for the purpose of clearing the title to the property or even of freeing the land itself from the dangerous ideas. The law orders that these be provided them in obedience to decisions of the judges and places the *Alcalde* as the agent of the reaction. The judgment for expulsion should be followed by the machine gun to do away with the resistance. My Government serves notice that this is not its policy, neither with respect to the campesino who has been dislodged nor with respect to the *colono* [squatter] who in good faith has invaded uncultivated lands in the belief that they were *baldíos* [in the public domain]. I do not want to make it the instrument of injustice, even though the injustice is supported by the provisions of the Codes. And that this policy has been effective is proved by the fact that many of these conflicts have disappeared without the proprietor's feeling less protected because the instruments needed to provoke them have been taken from him. But the present Administration does not desire to prolong indefinitely a situation harmful to the national economy. Property should be safeguarded in its use—not in its abuse—so that it will fulfill its social and economic function. In a country such as ours, lands, with extensions and limits fixed by law, should be acquired by two titles: by labor and by a public deed, without the latter giving immortal right to the possession of undeveloped lands. And the government desires that there be defined in this law how, when, and for what reasons one becomes proprietor, in order to prevent that property's being held by usurpers, and also in order to clarify the value of the titles of the *latifundista* who makes use of his domains and the value of the claims of the colono who with prodigious energies robs the jungle of a small tract on which to build a hut and raise a family.

❧ PART. II ❧

Current Agrarian Reform Programs in Latin America

Introductory Note

It has not been easy to select the few extracts that could be included in this small volume from among the welter of publications dealing with agrarian reform in Latin America which suddenly appeared after about 1950. Those that have been included are taken exclusively from the publications of Latin Americans, on the assumption that the writings of North Americans would be more readily accessible to the reader. Some materials were included to represent the position of the extreme Marxists, although the bulk of them were taken from those who champion a transformation of the social system from the old one which was centered about the large landed estate to one in which the family-sized farm is the core. The predominance of the latter is because most of the laws and programs actually in effect or under way, and most of the projects under serious study, are representative of this moderate ideological position. The other extreme, which many call the extreme Right, and which may differ from the Marxist ideal only in the single respect that the big estate is privately owned and operated and not state owned and operated, hardly figures in the publications. It gains expression, though, and very important expression at that, through action on the estates themselves, in the offices and clubs of the wealthy, and in the halls of the national parliaments.

Four of the selections deal with agrarian reform matters in Brazil. The first of these, prepared by studious José Arthur Rios, able sociologist and lawyer, who has been in the thick of the struggle for agrarian reform since 1950, traces the development of concern with agrarian reform in the Portuguese-speaking half of South America. The second is the "guide lines" prepared by the Commission on Agrarian Policy which was appointed by President Getúlio Vargas in 1952, and is a document which has had tremendous influence upon Brazilian thinking relative to agrarian reform. The third, by J. V. Freitas Marcondes, highly qualified sociologist and lawyer, sets forth many of the realities with respect to agrarian reform plans and projects in Brazil. To accompany these, the fourth is what might well be designated as the charter of Marxist-type agrarian reform proposals in Brazil. It is "The Declaration of Belo Horizonte," promulgated following a gathering in the capital of Minas Gerais which was organized and conducted by Francisco Julião, of "Peasant League" fame, and kindred spirits of pronounced leftist tendencies.

Bolivia's agrarian reform, which flared up and moved so quickly that the basic legislation on the subject may be considered ex post facto legalization of accomplished facts, provides the materials for three of the selections. Two of these are from the basic treatise on Bolivian Agrarian Law by José Flores Moncayo, and the third is from an excellent sociological study of the reform by the outstanding Bolivian sociologist, Eduardo Arze-Loureiro.

As agitation for agrarian reform gets under way in Chile, the Communists are stepping up their activities in the rural sections of that elongated country. From a small pamphlet written by Luis Corvalan, well-known Chilean Communist leader, which has been widely circulated in the rural districts, excerpts have been taken which illustrate the Party's tactics in agrarian reform matters in various Latin American countries.

In spite of all the publicity received by Castro's agrarian reform in Cuba, it is difficult or impossible to find succinct, objective, and germane materials that deal with the needs for, the objectives of, and the methods used in the reform. In the bibliographical section of the information supplied by Castro's delegation for use in the Seminar on Land Problems in Latin America (held at Montevideo, Uruguay, in

November and December, 1959, under the auspices of the Food and Agriculture Organization), there was only one title: *Rural Cuba* by Lowry Nelson! In view of this, excerpts from the Agrarian Reform Law as it was promulgated are offered as the best materials available. The extent to which the measures that were put into effect correspond, or fail to correspond, to the blueprint of the plans is a moot question that cannot as yet be answered in any satisfactory manner.

The Mexican agrarian revolution or reform has, of course, supplied the theme for most of what has been written about agrarian reform in Latin America by economists, sociologists, historians, and others in the United States. Even so, it would not be well to omit analyses of this important development, especially in its most recent phases, in a volume such as this. Therefore, two extracts have been selected and translated. One of them is a thumbnail sketch of the natural history of agrarian reform in Mexico, with emphasis upon current modifications, by the noted Mexican economist, Ramón Fernández y Fernández; the other is an exposition of the new phase in the reform by one of the officials of the agency in charge of agrarian reform activities, Víctor Manzanilla Schaffer.

Venezuela and Colombia are among the countries in which a moderate agrarian reform program is being pushed most vigorously. Colombian materials figure prominently in the Introduction and in Part I of this volume, but it has been deemed advisable to use in this section some materials which would indicate the nature of the work that the Venezuelans have under way. Accordingly, a section from Venezuela's Agrarian Reform Law of 1960, in which the objectives of the reform are specified, is included.

Because the general property tax is used so little throughout Latin America, idle or poorly used expanses of territory are encountered widely and even on the outskirts of great population centers. Under these circumstances serious Latin American thinkers frequently question the extent to which property ownership is actually performing a truly social function. It is difficult for anyone from outside the area to understand agrarian reform activities in Spanish America and Brazil without some knowledge of the basic thinking involved. Accordingly, the treatment of this topic which was prepared by Colombia's noted sociologist, Orlando Fals Borda, for use at the Seminar on Land Problems in Latin America, has been translated and included in this section.

The final selection is probably the only summary statement relating to agrarian reform ever prepared as the result of extensive exchange of views and intensive discussion on the part of experts from various parts of Latin America and a few of their fellows in the United States and Great Britain. It came out of a meeting of "high level experts in agricultural problems" which was held at the Pan American Union in Washington, D. C., in October, 1961, under the auspices of the Inter-American Committee for Agricultural Development. The over-all view of the principal features of agrarian reform plans and proposals for Latin America which came out of this meeting makes a fitting conclusion for Part II of this volume and for the book itself.

6

THE DEVELOPMENT OF INTEREST IN AGRARIAN REFORM IN BRAZIL

José Arthur Rios

꙰

It was after 1930 that we in Brazil began to speak of the agrarian problem. Prior to this, the country man was merely a literary theme. But when the economic crisis projected itself upon the political scene and later, as a chasm appeared between the form of the State and the economic structure of the nation through the influx of the revolutionary ideologies of Marxism and Fascism, the expressions "rural problem" and "agrarian question" came to be legal tender in the press and in the parliamentary tribune. In this same epoch we came to know of the European agrarian reforms effected, often with disastrous results, following the First World War.

With the coffee crisis, the decadence of the fountains of production, and the steady migration to the cities, the Brazilian conscience came to think of the situation of the coun-

Translated from the Introduction by José Arthur Rios in José Arthur Rios, ed., *Recomendações sôbre Reforma Agrária* (Rio de Janeiro: Instituto Brasileiro de Ação Democrática, 1961), pp. xi-xvii. Printed by permission of the publisher.

try man as a "problem" and to seek solutions to it. These were, as a general rule, as simple as the diagnoses that were made. Some sought to augment transportation facilities; for many, the opening of roads was national salvation; and others struggled for large-scale campaigns to overcome illiteracy.

Political events of this decade resulted in a still greater accentuation, in Brazilian public opinion, of the importance of the rural masses and of the necessity for a series of measures that would integrate them into the national communion. The *caipira* thus ceased to be a literary theme and became a headache. An old expression, the lack of arms[1] regained circulation and came to be the maximal manifestation, the gravest symptom, of the crisis.

The expression is characteristic. It reveals the angle from which the problem was confronted. It was an attempt to instill new life into a declining system of production. The country man counted because of his place in the machinery of production. It was a repetition, in a more apprehensive tone and given prestige by the apparatus of a language that sought to be scientific, of a form of stating the problem which came from the days of the Empire and the mouths of slave-owning planters. It dismembered man himself and thought of his problems in terms of the arm, more important in this case than the head, the stomach, or even the spirit.

This rural crisis, for which there was an appeal for reform, is only one aspect of Brazil's general crisis, and it marks a moment of transition in our capitalism. While the cities grow and industry develops at a rate which seeks to keep pace with the movements of the international market and in line with universal patterns—universal within the capitalistic area—of technical efficiency and intensive production, Brazilian agriculture and the Brazilian countryside remain bound to feudalistic forms of society and economy, to ways of doing and thinking characteristic of the precapitalistic era in which they originated.

---

[1] Lack of hands is the English equivalent. [Ed.]

There are in the Brazilian agrarian problem, therefore, forces as old as the country itself, and recent influxes which result, here as in other economically underdeveloped areas, from the expansion of capitalism throughout the world and the struggle for hegemony of the markets. The study of some of these is the thread that leads us to the heart of the problem and which can indicate to us, better than any deduction based upon abstract models, the way toward a Brazilian agrarian reform.

The expression is new, but the idea is old. Throughout history it is interwoven with Brazilian liberal thought. It is encountered, by a coincidence that it is unnecessary to belabor, in the writings of those who advocated the abolition of slavery, unrestricted immigration, and an entire series of social and political reforms. The idea is in the works of José Bonifácio. It is in those of Tavares Bastos and Joaquim Nabuco, in the Messages of the presidents of the provinces, and in the Reports of Imperial Times, always associated with the great problem of colonization.

José Bonifácio did not think merely of establishing colonies [i.e., settlements of small landholders] on lands granted to the workers in the Ipanema iron factory; he dreamed of the transformation of the regime of agricultural landholding, with the replacement of the latifundium by a subdivision of the land in such a way as "to favor the colonization by poor Europeans, Indians, mulattoes, and free Negroes." [2]

The ideas of Tavares Bastos about immigration and colonization are found disseminated throughout various writings. Moreover, he did not dissociate them from a land law capable of creating the conditions necessary for Brazil to receive great contingents of immigrants and colonists. "One of the major obstacles to spontaneous immigration is the fact that great proprietors possess vast expanses of the best land, lands that are close to the markets and to the roads. In addition, this fatal result of the unintelligent system of

[2] After Octavio Tarquinio de Souza, *História dos Fundadores do Império do Brasil: I. José Bonifácio* (Rio de Janeiro: José Olímpio, 1957), pp. 66, 130, and 136.

grants used without restriction by the central government is also an obstacle in the way of the development of free labor." [3] The "agrarian reform" which he proposed in the *Memorial Relating to Immigration,* written in 1867, was based upon the distribution of the national domain, the advertising and sale of unalienated land, the alienation of public land, and a land tax.

Joaquim Nabuco never dissociated the abolition of the slaves and the appearance of a class of free small farmers. In various places in his book on abolition he repeatedly expresses the following thought: "An important class, whose development is impeded by slavery, is that of the landless farmers and the generality of the country people and those of the *sertão.*" [4] Throughout this admirable book, a thoroughly modern sociological document and the testimonial of a conscience, one encounters two associated ideas: the suppression of slavery and the struggle against the latifundia.

> The truth is that the vast areas exploited by colonial slavery have a uniform aspect of sorrow and abandonment: in them there is no partnership of man and land, no features of permanent habitation, no signs of natural growth [. . .] . The population has no definitive possession of the soil: the great proprietor conquered it from nature by means of his slaves, used it, and extended his domain; later he failed because of the extravagance which almost always results from a fortune acquired in a bad way, and finally, worn out and exhausted, the soil returned to nature.[5]

For the most outstanding representatives of this liberal school of thought the social effects of slavery could be fully eradicated only by the distribution of the ownership of the soil to the freedmen, by immigration, and by colonization on a large scale.

---

[3] A. C. Tavares Bastos, *Os Males do Presente e as Esperanças do Futuro* (São Paulo: Companhia Editora Nacional, 1939), p. 87.

[4] Joaquim Nabuco, *O Abolicionismo* (London: Abraham Kingdom, 1883), p. 177.

[5] *Ibid.,* p. 149.

Likewise, foreign visitors who traveled throughout our territory, from the dawn of our independence, placed the problem of Brazil's development in the same setting. Thus Saint Hilaire, a sociologist of the future, *prior to 1822* already looked forward to a land system that would be able to sustain the rural population of Brazil and raise it above the misery of slavery.

All of this indicates a lack of originality by which the discussion has been out of date for at least a century. Brazil, which might have led America in a powerful movement to reform the structure, is still debating problems that have been solved in most places. There is nothing more striking than the tenaciousness with which the Brazilian political elite, with the most specious motives, has postponed this social reform, subordinating the well-being of the country to the interests of their class. This opposition, this blind but purposeful resistance, has been the big factor in retarding the solution of the Brazilian agrarian problem.

The secret ballot, giving political importance to the rural electorate, was another important conquest which gave relief to the human problem of the country man. Even though boss control of the vote may not have disappeared entirely, a function and result of misery in the open country, its effects were diminished and a freer expression was given to the ballot of the son of the soil.

Timidly, there were included in Articles 147 and 156 of the 1946 Constitution the dispositions which some consider to be the first attempt to reform the statutes pertaining to land. Thus, for example, they were so considered in the Message sent in 1947 by the President, General Eurico Gaspar Dutra, to the National Congress: "The fundamental lines of this proposed agrarian reform will be prudently inspired in its reality and will encounter its initial form in Articles 147 and 156 of the Constitution." [6] Many, nevertheless, understand that by making social well-being a condition for the use of property (Article 147) the Constitu-

---

[6] Sociedade Nacional de Agricultura, *Reforma Agrária* (Rio de Janeiro, 1947), p. 10.

tion took a forward step; but by prescribing prior indemnification in cash for expropriations (Article 141, paragraph 16) it withdrew the benefits that might have been harvested from that general principle. Relative to Article 156, merely programmatic, it deals principally with matters related to colonization and the use of public lands, with no major consequences for the elaboration of an agrarian law actually worthy of the name.

In this period the first projects for an agrarian law came forward in Congress. In 1947 Deputy Nestor Duarte produced his brief and lucid project "Concerning the Regime of Farming Arable Lands, and the Classification of These Lands and the Use of These Lands for Cultivation, Stockraising, and Dwellings, the Regulation of the Conditions of Sharecropping and Renting, and Giving Other Provisions." In 1948, the Minister of Agriculture, Daniel de Carvalho, sent to President Dutra and the latter to Congress the draft of the Agrarian Law that was prepared by Dr. Afranio de Carvalho. In sending this proposed law to the President of the Republic, the Minister characterized its general orientation in the following manner: "It does not attempt [. . .] either to socialize the land or to destroy private property, but to fulfill the prescriptions of Articles 147 and 156 of the Constitution, by means of a long-range policy of land use, principally of public lands and of those that may receive the benefits of great projects for reclamation and improvement."

Other projects of greater or lesser scope followed, some with the dimensions of true Rural Codes, and others intended to deal with specific aspects of the subject, such as financing, credit, social security, and social work.

More important than the number and quality of these projects is the fact that *none of them* was successful in securing presidential sanction. By means of a tacit compromise the government and the opposition left these projects to sleep in the dust of the parliamentary archives.

This did not forestall the fact that all of the political parties came to include the theme of agrarian reform in their programs. Likewise, all presidential candidates came to include planks on this subject in their electoral platforms. Fitted in between aid to productivity and protection for the worker, in an order of placement that varied with the Party, there was the reform of the Land Statute.

In July, 1951, João Cleofas, a Minister in the Government of Getúlio Vargas, established the National Commission on Agrarian Policy, for the purpose of studying and proposing to the President of the Republic the measures judged to be necessary for the organization and development of the agricultural economy and for rural welfare, as well as analyzing the projects related to the reform of agricultural legislation and access to the land itself (Decree 29,803 of July 27, 1951, Articles 1 and 2, single paragraph). Also in 1951, the Executive sent to Congress a project instituting the Rural Social Service. In this way were created the administrative instruments of the reform, although they lacked their definitive configuration.

In April, 1961, President Janio Quadros decided to establish a working group to elaborate a Land Statute.

7

GUIDE LINES FOR AN AGRARIAN REFORM IN BRAZIL

The National Commission on Agrarian Policy

❧

From the experiences of other countries that have agrarian structures similar to that of Brazil, and from the new social meaning given by modern constitutions, including that of Brazil, to property rights to the land, there arise some general guide lines that should prevail in our agrarian reform. These include the following fundamental points.

I. Basic Principles:

1. The Brazilian Constitution states in Article 147 that the use of property shall be conditioned by the social well-being and that the law shall promote a just distribution of property with equal opportunity for all.

2. The fundamental objective of agrarian reform in Brazil is to offer access to property to those who work the soil, so as to prevent the proletarization of the rural masses and eliminate the effects of uneconomical and antisocial use of the land.

Translated from Comissão Nacional de Política Agrária, *Diretrizes para una Reforma Agrária no Brasil*, Mimeographed (Rio de Janeiro: Comissão Nacional de Política Agrária, 1952), pp. 1-3.

3. Simultaneously with the subdivision of *latifundia* and the consolidation of *minifundia*, the agrarian reform shall also take care to valorize the man and the land, so as to guarantee to all work that will make possible an honorable existence.

II. Concerning the Agrarian Regime:

1. Legislation pertaining to lands shall take into account, as much as possible, the customs and traditions of each region.

2. Agricultural legislation should provide minimal conditions that would make it possible for the small farm to carry on its social and productive functions.

3. Lands should not be subdivided indiscriminately, when, because of the nature of the crops and the type of agricultural production, this would result in the economic decline of a region.

III. Forms and Systems of Expropriation:

1. Indemnification for the expropriation of unproductive latifundia should avoid the rule of Article 141, paragraph 16 of the Federal Constitution and be based upon Article 147, even though, perhaps, a constitutional amendment may be necessary.

2. The expropriation of land in the social interest should exclude from the indemnity payments of any kind except those corresponding to the principal, the improvements, and a reasonable interest on the money invested.

3. A subdivision of lands adjacent to or near the cities is obligatory when, because of their extent and the use to which they are put, they constitute an obstacle to the development of agriculture and do not help satisfy the exigencies of supplying the urban area.

4. The following lands should be considered as most subject to expropriation:

(a) those which remain uncultivated, despite the fact that conditions favor their permanent use;

(b) those that manifestly are poorly cultivated in a technical sense, including those which, although located favorably with respect to public irrigation projects, are not being irrigated;

(c) those which, acquired for speculative purposes, remain unused.

5. Lands whose values will be increased as a result of large public projects, which constitute latifundia whose improvement depends almost exclusively upon such projects, and which are subject to economic use by means of agricultural colonization, shall be expropriated before the projects are undertaken. There shall be reserved for the owner whose lands have been expropriated an area equal in size to that previously maintained in permanent cultivation.

6. Areas near urban centers, the cultivation of which is essential for the supply of such centers, may not be subdivided into building lots, or if they should be, they shall be obliged to follow a plan of agricultural zoning.

IV. Colonization:

1. [There should be] unity in legislation and a central administrative agency for all colonization activities. [There should be] a careful selection of lands in accordance with the factors which guarantee a fixation of man to the land and the development of production.

2. Priority should be given to rich lands, healthful and near the centers of consumption, so that the population will give preference to natural expansion rather than to a transplantation to isolated zones, irrespective of how fertile the latter may be said to be.

3. In colonization the effort should be made to maintain an equilibrium between lands suitable for grazing and those suitable for agriculture.

V. Agricultural Credit:

1. Credit by official agencies should be oriented so as actually to benefit the small farmer. For this purpose the essential condition is to decentralize credit to the maximum, eliminating the bureaucratic obstacles, and to make the guarantees demanded less harsh.

2. As a general rule, credit by official agencies should be extended in cash, as well as, under certain conditions, in machines, implements, seeds, fertilizers, and livestock, along with the necessary technical assistance.

3. Preference should be given to supplying credit

through agricultural cooperatives, thus intensifying personal credit.

VI. *General Dispositions:*

1. The adequate imposition of taxes upon property (land tax, transmission tax, etc.) constitutes a means of discouraging the unproductive possession of the soil. When, as is the case in Brazil, these tributes are the prerogative of the states, it is essential that there be an inter-state agreement, under the auspices of the federal government, for the purpose of securing uniform provisions with respect to incidence and rates, always with due respect to the distinctive features of each unit of the Federation.

2. Provisions should be included in the agrarian reform law for stimulating, in every way possible, the proprietors of rural establishments to invest their profits in building up and improving the soil. Therefore, the estates that through exemplary management are technically and economically efficient are not to be expropriated.

3. [Efforts shall be made] to develop the small property in economically sound ways, particularly in the zones surrounding the cities, so as to establish among the agricultural enterprises the system of small horticultural farms and diversified farms.

4. There should be established, in each productive zone, the minimum size of the property, beyond which subdivision will not be permitted, even by inheritance.

5. [Programs should be developed] to promote, throughout all parts of the interior, the creation of rural cooperatives of all types, as well as organizations of proprietors and laborers of all classes, granting them favors and gifts.

6. [Measures should be taken] to eliminate or ease the taxes upon newly established rural industries.

7. [Efforts should be made] to orient our system of taxation so as to eliminate or reduce tariffs and duties on exports which increase the costs of living and production of the agriculturists.

8. The agrarian reform should set as an objective the creation of rural communities capable of progressing economically, socially, and politically within Brazilian society.

❧

8

SALIENT FEATURES OF
AGRARIAN REFORM
PROPOSALS IN BRAZIL

J. V. Freitas Marcondes

❧

During the last twenty years or, more exactly, following the Second World War, the expression "agrarian reform" has received special attention in nearly all parts of the world. Never was a *reform* so discussed and debated, in Brazil or outside of it, as the *agrarian*. At first the appearance of an article or pamphlet on the subject was a novelty, then the books began to flow, and now we are in the epoch of indexes and bibliographies of the publications dealing with this controversial subject. Recently, the Institute of Social Sciences of the University of Brazil published a bibliography listing 1,164 titles, with a geographical index that included 61 countries, regions, and continents and giving the names of 787 authors and institutions that have published on agrarian reform and related matters.[1] Serious journals and

Translated from J. V. Freitas Marcondes, "Reforma Agrária à Luz das Ciências Sociais," *Sociologia* (São Paulo), XXIV (no. 4, 1962), 273-285. Printed by permission of the publisher.

[1] Evaristo de Morais Filho, *Bibliográfia sôbre Reforma Agrária* (Rio de Janeiro: Universidade do Brasil, 1962). We must em-

reviews have dedicated special numbers to the subject.[2] Congresses and seminars have been organized for the specific purpose of discussing the problem.[3] In Brazil's National Congress up to 1958 no less than 213 projects had been introduced dealing with agrarian reform and related topics;[4] and by the present time we believe that this number has already risen to more than 300.

[. . .] There are two principal reasons [. . .] for the appearance and continued aggravation of the problem: (a) an increasing haphazard industrialization; and (b) an overwhelming feudal agrarian structure that is almost completely out of line with prevailing social theories relative to the social function of property. [. . .]

The phenomenon of industrialization is an old one. It began in the middle of the eighteenth century, with progress in technology, or what then was called the "Industrial Revolution." This revolution, which began in England, and which alarmed the scholars, gave rise to waves of discontent and an overwhelming phenomenon of urbanization. [. . .] Two centuries later, this Industrial Revolution struck Brazil, bringing with it the same consequences, that is, the depopulation of the countryside and the building of urban anthills. The principal industrial centers of Brazil, led by São Paulo, tripled in population in less than fifty years. [. . .]

---

phasize that even this publication did not include many important titles, as for example, and to cite only the case of the scholarly José Arthur Rios, "Rumo da Reforma Agrária," *Arquivos do Instituto de Direito Social*, X (1952), 57-74; and "Modifição da Estrutura Agrária do Nordeste," *Seminário para o Desenvolvimento do Nordeste, Anais*, II (1959), 295-345; and other works of the same author.

[2] *Arquivos do Instituto de Direito Social* (São Paulo), X, (no. 1, 1952); *Revista Brasileira de Estudos Políticos* (Belo Horizonte), (no. 12, 1961); and *Revista do Conselho Nacional de Economia* (Rio de Janeiro), XI (1962).

[3] José Arthur Rios, ed., *Recomendações sôbre Reforma Agrária* (Rio de Janeiro: Instituto Brasileira de Ação Democrática, 1961).

[4] J. V. Freitas Marcondes, *Revisão e Reforma Agrária (Quatro Estudos)* (São Paulo: Instituto dos Advogados de São Paulo, 1962), p. 45.

According to all indications very few persons, even among those who direct our affairs, have perceived that the "monkey wrench" involved in Brazil's socio-economic crisis is our defective agrarian structure. The members of the ruling elite, the "proprietors" of the country, are the owners of immense expanses of land; and the great majority of them maintain their estates in an undeveloped condition, unproductive and perhaps paying no taxes. This is the enrooted remnant of the patriarchalism of two centuries ago, which gathered all power, including the political, into its hands. About a year ago, we attempted to obtain some data from the members of the Brazilian Congress in order to learn how many of them were landowners, and the size, use, and production of their properties. It is hardly necessary to indicate that we had to abandon our endeavor. Nevertheless, I am of the opinion that very few of these "politicians," most of whom have captive seats in the National Congress, are acquainted with a book which described the grave defects of Cuba's agrarian structure. This book was based upon rigorous field work and was written by one of the most distinguished sociologists in the United States, Lowry Nelson, former head of the Department of Rural Sociology at the University of Minnesota. Without resorting to demagoguery or to moralizing, this sociologist demonstrated that in Cuba, well before Fidel Castro, a few families owned almost all of the Island and that the great majority of the people were laborers or landless families.

Cuban society, as we have said, can more easily be classified into two groups only, upper and lower—or perhaps it would not be too inaccurate to say those who hire servants and those who do not; or, if one wishes, those who work with their hands and those who work with their heads, or do not work at all. The latter are the heirs of the old aristocracy, the former, the heirs of their serfs or slaves. The one group scorned work with their hands, the others were "to the manor born." This simple dichotomy of "upper" and "lower" is based primarily on a tradition, on socio-psychological factors, rather than on differences in income and wealth, which are secondary criteria[. . .].[5]

Without fear of erring, we can state that, with the exception of southern Brazil, the remainder of our country constitutes a carbon copy of the situation in Cuba prior to the Castro revolution. I believe that if it had not been for the extremely heavy internal migration from the Northeast and other regions to the developed South, which is looked upon, longed for, and desired as a land of Canaan, even now we should have other conflicts [. . .] much more serious than those of Engenho Galiléia, Santa Fé do Sul, Planaltina, Porecatú, Palmas, Chopinzinho, etc.

With reference to agrarian reform we also must not fail to think of the feudalistic agrarian structure that is dominant in most of the states, whose lands are still lacking a well-executed cadastral survey; nor of the little that is known of the quality of these lands. These points are fundamental, but, even so, they are included in none of the projects under consideration by the National Congress. [. . .]

Much more grave than the lack of data about privately owned lands is the ignorance, almost complete, of the tremendous expanses of land which belong to the states and to the Nation. In the State of São Paulo alone, we know of the existence of about 2,200,000 hectares of unused public domain. [. . .] Therefore, we cannot help concluding that, with respect to Brazil's agrarian structure, the greatest feudal lord is the public itself, including the State of São Paulo. The public domain includes millions of hectares of undeveloped land, which brings no returns of any kind for the public coffers, and which awakens the justifiable desire for possession by those who wish to farm and who lack even the smallest piece of land. In this case the public power itself is the largest nonconformist with the consecrated principle of Article 147 of the Federal Constitution: "The use of property shall be conditioned to the social welfare." The

---

[5] Lowry Nelson, *Rural Cuba* (Minneapolis: University of Minnesota Press, 1950), p. 159.

big criminal, therefore, is the public power itself which concurs in and aggravates the social conflicts, by failing to distribute its lands, by not increasing the production of foodstuffs, and in this way by augmenting the inflation and other evils which the people are already beginning to feel with dismay. Happily, some of the state governors already appreciate the magnitude of the crisis and, as a result, are presently thinking of the distribution of some portions of the state lands, as in the case of the governors of São Paulo, Goiás, and Mato Grosso. In other regions, principally in the Northeast, the Catholic Church is attempting to correct the evil.

Brazilian social scientists know and denounce these evils, but, unfortunately, in the hour of the elaboration of the agrarian reform, they are inexcusably put on the sidelines by the "hidden forces," as some say, but forces which are clearly and easily seen by the naked eye, as we are attempting to demonstrate.

During April, 1961, the Instituto Brasileiro de Ação Democrática held an important seminar in the city of Rio de Janeiro, in which 34 specialists participated, for the specific purpose of studying and discussing the problem of agrarian reform in Brazil. From the many angles in whose light materials were studied and debated came information relative to the best type of reform for our country.

On the basis of the work of Bandini,[6] who planned and administered the Italian agrarian reform, known varieties of agrarian reform, all seeking the modification of agrarian structures and the increase of agricultural production, were classified into five types. These, along with some of the subtypes, are as follows: (1) *Radical*, based on a collective agrarian system, including the totalitarian, state type of Russia, and the non-totalitarian type of Israel; (2) *Subdivisionist*, the promotion in various ways of the subdivision of large estates, such as took place in Central Europe, the Balkans, and Greece following the First World War; (3) *Gradual*

---

[6] Mário Bandini, *La Riforma Fondiaria* (Roma: Edizioni 5 Lune, 1956).

and Indirect, involving an indirect and slow process of transformation in the agrarian structure, as in Great Britain; (4) *Transformationist,* such as the reforms taking place in Arabic and Oriental countries, wherein the units of cultivation are small and almost always operated by tenants; and (5) *Betterment,* seeking the subdivision of the land accompanied by intensive activities designed to improve both man and the land, as in Italy, Holland, Finland, etc.

The editor of the proceedings[7] of the Seminar mentioned above regrouped these five types, "according to the mentality prevailing in their execution," into three: (1) *Conservative* reforms, or pseudo reforms, which attempt to avoid the genuine problem of change in structure and lose themselves in tangential measures for rendering assistance of a paternal nature; (2) *Totalitarian* types of reforms, such as the Russian or the Chinese; and (3) *Democratic* reforms.

After a description of each of these three types in which it was emphasized that, in Brazil, projects of the first type predominate, measures "defined by some large landowners as assistance to agriculture, agricultural credit, the increase of agricultural production, or the stimulus to colonization, and almost always presented under nationalistic slogans such as the fixation of man upon the land and support for the native settler," and after condemning reforms of the totalitarian type, this report urged reform of the democratic type. It sought to characterize this amply as follows:

> The democratic reform, oriented toward the common welfare and a policy of social justice, envisions neither a class struggle nor the primacy of the economic factor. It lacks confidence in the omnipotence of the State and seeks to avoid such by strengthening private initiative and that of associations. Its purpose is neither the subversion of classes, nor, primarily, an increase in production, but the improvement of man. Its objective, therefore, is not the mass expropriation of the lands [held in a manner] that constitutes a grave

---

[7] Rios, *Recomendações sôbre Reforma Agrária,* p. 316.

social injustice, nor the confiscation of land by the State, a measure that, in countries of totalitarian tendencies such as Brazil where state paternalism ever tends to increase, will result in the oppression of the human being. The democratic agrarian reform seeks the concession of property rights to the land to the largest possible number of persons who are prepared to cultivate it, and, in this way, to diffuse among the rural masses the qualities of security, independence, and responsibility, which are lacking in the passive multitudes of the interior, and which characterize throughout the entire world the historic mission of the rural middle class. In order for the land to comply with its function, it is not necessary for the State to arrogate direct ownership to itself. It is sufficient to invoke the right of eminent domain of the soil and the right of intervention for the purpose of preventing maladjustments and injustices. It is in accordance with these principles that the agrarian reform should be made.[8]

From the above quotations and concepts one arrives at the conclusion that the Seminar mentioned sought, through a democratic agrarian reform, to create in our country a *rural middle class* to replace the prevailing system, which is to say, of what amounts almost to a system of social pariahs, who constitute the majority of the Brazilian population and an elevated percentage of that of the other Latin American countries, all of them likewise lacking agrarian reforms, and, in the majority of cases, lacking the "courage" to make them.

Various formulas have been advanced for the formation and development of the rural middle class, including some agrarian reform projects which rest in the National Congress. Nevertheless, as we see it, we shall never have a genuine, productive, and happy rural middle class if we do not take care to get a combination of landownership and the capacity to work; if we do not awaken in the rural man an ambition for progress, materially, physically, and intellectu-

[8] *Ibid.*, p. 318.

ally. It is not enough to place a man on a well-equipped farm, with house, water, and light; with contour curves and registered seeds; with tractors and fertilizers. Much more is needed than all of this. It is necessary to form a mentality, a personality adjusted to the rural environment and capable of understanding that this man and the members of his family, in addition to being landowners and trained producers, are also the ones who do the planning and perform the labor involved in their agricultural and stockraising activities. Each dynamic family cell should combine the three basic functions: those of the owner, the laborer, and the manager, in accordance with the formula of the maestro of the Sociology of Rural Life, Lynn Smith.[. . .] [9]

The great difference between Brazilian agriculture and that practiced in Lynn Smith's country [the United States] —the goal which we should attempt to achieve—is not to be viewed merely in terms of land actually cultivated, there 188 million hectares and here only 50 million. For the difference is also related to the average amount of land worked per person, there 8 hectares and here only 1; to the percentage of the population which depends upon agricultural activities for a livelihood, there less than 10 per cent and here more than 60 per cent; and to the implements used in the work, there the tractor and here the hoe. Moreover, it is relative to social and family type which works the land, there the "farmer" is a genuine representative of the middle social class, performing with the members of his family, and assisted only by them, the three functions mentioned above (those of owner, manager, and laborer), living on the farm and cultivating it completely, whereas here only one fifth of the rural population is made up of owners, a large percentage of whom are absentees, who relegate the work to the four fifths of the people who lack land and have small likelihood of obtaining any of it. On the other hand a large share of the Brazilians who own land are not prepared to cultivate it, or more correctly some are landowners and some

[9] See T. Lynn Smith, *Current Social Trends and Problems in Latin America* (Gainesville: University of Florida Press, 1957).

are laborers, but they lack the managerial capacity which, in the opinion of Louis Bromfield, is the most important of the trinity. Therefore, for the harmonious combination of these three factors of production it is necessary to consider the important role of education as the moving element in agrarian reform.

In the important field of education—especially in relation to agrarian reform—among us practically everything remains to be done. The teacher needs special training to enable him to understand the importance of that which he transmits and how this new message is to help bring about changes in the social structure and the better development of the rural man and his family; he also needs to know the community and to be grounded in the means and purposes of the reform philosophy. He must become convinced that the new knowledge which he is transmitting constitutes the principal factor in the success of an agrarian reform. He should become a practical and idealistic reformer, complementing the work of the agronomist, the agricultural extension worker, and of other technicians, as has been done in Mexico since 1910. The school itself must be planned for the specific purpose of dynamizing and accelerating not only the students, but the family and the community itself; it must be the center of irradiation of the movement, by means of the new system of apprenticeship. The school programs have to be developed in relation to the environment, and not upon national bases that are uniform and rigid as are the programs of the totalitarian countries. It is necessary and even indispensable for the school and the teacher to have the competence and the authority necessary to experiment and even to make alterations in the program, which is to say that flexibility should be the fundamental characteristic of the school, the program, and the teacher. [. . .]

Perhaps the major obstacle to the reform philosophy will not be the problem of the teacher, of the program, or of the school, but that of the directors, many of them still of an antiquated mentality and even uninformed about the abc's of the reform. On the other hand, the majority of the politicians and the "technicians" who elaborate agrarian reform projects completely forget the important part which education must play, as though it were possible to accomplish reform of this type without the collaboration of the school, the teacher, or in the final analysis, of education. Whoever wishes to take the trouble to force himself to examine the innumerable projects which propose to reform Brazilian rural life will certainly encounter this unpardonable gap in the majority of them. [. . .]

In any study of agrarian reform, one must not fail to speak of agricultural credit. If education constitutes the fundamental foundation stone of the reform, the system of credit is another of the principal bases upon which it must rest. Without a well-planned, well-organized, and well-administered system of agricultural credit—with less favoritism and less politics—our production will continue to be deficient. But we are saying nothing new. However, few people know that in our state [São Paulo], which is considered a leader in almost all respects, if we add all the loans made by the departments of agricultural credit of the Bank of Brazil, the Bank of the State, and all of the private banks in the state, we shall find that for the year 1961 not even 1 per cent of the recipients were farmers. Much more important than the insignificant 1 per cent, we will be struck by the fact that almost all of these loans were made to politicians, who, generally speaking, were not in need of them. These agricultural loan departments or their equivalents still live under the system of "big shots," with extremely rare exceptions. Caio Prado, Jr., in a recent article,[1] stated that in the rice-growing section of the São Francisco Valley, a certain landowner, who was financed by the Bank of Brazil with interest at 6 per cent, "advanced" to a sharecropper the amount of CR$3,750 to collect three months later CR$5,000, or, in other words, at an interest of 33 per cent.

---

[1] "Nova Contribução para a Análise da Questão Agrária no Brasil," *Revista Brasiliense*, no. 43 (Setembro-Outubro, 1962), 11-52.

9

THE DECLARATION OF
BELO HORIZONTE
Francisco Julião et al.

In the closing session of the work of the First National Congress of Farmers and Agricultural Laborers, in Belo Horizonte, attended by 1,600 delegates from all parts of the nation, a large mass of the people, and representatives of the workers, of the intellectuals, of the students, and of government officials, including the President and the Prime Minister of the Republic, the following Resolution was unanimously approved:

The oppressed and exploited rural masses of our country, assembled in this National Congress, make manifest through this Resolution their unalterable decision to fight for a radical agrarian reform. Such an agrarian reform has nothing to do with the palliative measures proposed by the backward forces of the nation, whose objective is to put off still longer the liquidation of latifundiary estates. The banner of a radi-

Translated from the text as published in Francisco Julião, *Que São as Ligas Camponesas?* Cadernos do Povo Brasileiro, no. 1 (Rio de Janeiro: Editôra Civilização Brasileira, S. A., 1962), Anexo B, pp. 81-87. Printed by permission of the publisher.

cal agrarian reform is the only standard capable of uniting and organizing the national forces which desire the welfare and happiness of the masses of rural laborers and the progress of Brazil.

The First National Congress of Farmers and Agricultural Laborers, following the debates carried on throughout the entire period in which it has been assembled, defined the basic elements which characterize the present situation of the rural masses and established the general principles on which a radical agrarian reform may be based.

The strong predominance of the latifundium is the principal characteristic of the present agrarian situation in Brazil. With a rural population of about 38 millions, there are in Brazil only 2,065,000 agricultural properties. In this number are included 70,000 latifundia, which represent only 3.39 per cent of the existing agricultural establishments but which include 62.33 per cent of the total occupied area of the country. This monopolization of the land, along with foreign colonizing capital, especially the North American, is the basis for a domination of Brazilian political life and a great exploitation of Brazil's riches. This monopolization of the land is responsible for the low productivity of our agriculture, for the high cost of living, and for all the antiquated, retrograde, and extremely burdensome forms of a semi-feudal type of production which enslave and brutalize millions of landless peasants. This outmoded, backward, barbarous, and inhuman agrarian structure constitutes a decisive barrier to national development and is one of the most evident forms of an internal process of spoilation.

In order to overcome the present condition of chronic underdevelopment, of profound economic, political, and social instability, and above all to deter the growing misery and the increasing starvation and to elevate the low level of living of the people in general and to improve the unbearable conditions of life and work to which the rural masses are submitted, it becomes daily more and more urgent and imperative to accomplish an agrarian reform which will modify *radically* the present structure of our agricultural economy and the social relationships which rule in the countryside.

This agrarian reform cannot be successful unless it begins with an immediate rupture and the most complete liquidation of the monopoly of the land exercised by the retrograde forces of the latifundium and the consequent establishment of free and easy access to the land on the part of those who want to cultivate it.

It is equally necessary that the agrarian reform shall satisfy the most basic necessities and demands of the country people. This is to say it should correspond to the vital anxieties and interests of those who work the land and who here are found assembled, in the persons of their representatives and delegates, from throughout the entire nation in the First National Congress of Farmers and Agricultural Laborers of Brazil.

For the men who work the land, agrarian reform, that is a complete and just solution of our country's agricultural problem, is the only way to resolve effectively the grave problem discussed by the rural masses, and therefore they, more than any other part of the Brazilian population, are interested in its realization. The rural masses understand that the final solution of the problem rests with them.

The execution of an agrarian reform, effectively democratic and progressive, can be attained only by means of vigorous, organized, and decisive action by the masses of rural laborers, aided fraternally in their struggle by the city proletariat, the students, the intellectuals, and the other nationalistic and democratic forces of the Brazilian people.

The methods proposed here, genuinely capable of leading to the solution of the huge problem of agrarian reform in our country, obviously will collide with and be opposed by the interests and solutions of those social forces which are favored by and prosper through the maintenance of the present archaic and noxious agrarian structure. Upon this structure reposes the unstable economy, dependent and underdeveloped, of our country, whose modification these forces seek to prevent at all costs.

The agrarian reform which we propose and defend differs from and opposes frontally, however, the innumerable projects, indications, and proposals relative to the pretended "reforms," agricultural revisions, and other elaborate maneuvers presented by the representatives of those forces whose interests and objectives correspond above all to the desire to maintain the essentials of the present state of affairs indefinitely.

The agrarian reform for which we fight has as its fundamental objective the complete liquidation of the monopoly of the land by the latifundium, the basis of the antieconomic and antisocial relationships which prevail in the rural areas and which are the principal obstacles to the free and prosperous agrarian development of the nation.

For the purpose of accomplishing an agrarian reform of genuine interest to the people and the masses of rural workers, we believe it is urgent and indispensable to solve the following problems:

(a)—A radical transformation of the present agrarian structure of the country, with the liquidation of the monopoly of property rights to the land exercised by the latifundistas, principally by means of the expropriation of the latifundia by the Federal Government, and the replacement of the monopolization of property in land by ownership by the rural masses, either private or through associations, and by ownership by the State.

(b)—Maximal access to the possession and use of the soil by those who wish to till it, by means of sale or lease at moderate prices of the lands expropriated from the large owners and the free distribution of public lands.

In addition to these methods, which seek to modify radically the present bases of the agrarian problem in those aspects which involve the land question, solutions are essential which will produce an improvement in the actual conditions of life and labor of the rural masses, such as:

(a)—Respect for the full, free, and democratic right of the rural masses to organize independently in their class associations.

(b)—Effective application of the part of existing labor legislation which pertains to agricultural laborers, as well as

immediate measures by the government to impede viola-
tions of the same; and the elaboration of a statute which en-
visages adequate labor legislation for the rural workers.

(c)—Full guarantee of free and autonomous unioniza-
tion of the rural wage earners and semi–wage earners. Immediate recognition of rural labor unions.

(d)—Immediate and effective aid for the small farmers'
economy in all of its forms.

The rural masses are conscious of the worsening, with
each passing day, of the unbearable weight of the situation
to which they are subjected. For this reason they are mo-
bilizing and organizing to fight resolutely in order to attain
their objectives, as these are expressed in an effective, democratic, and patriotic agrarian reform. This struggle is already
under way and it will continue until the objectives, for
whose realization the rural masses will not spare their efforts
nor measure their sacrifices, are attained.

Under present conditions everything should be done to
see that the forces that direct the destinies of the Brazilian
nation are devoting themselves to the accomplishment of an
effective and unpostponable agrarian policy. This should be
capable of starting with the execution of partial measures
and proceeding to the solution of the problems that are essential for the full realization of the agrarian reform which
is needed by the farmers and the agricultural laborers, as
well as by the entire Brazilian people. Such measures,
among others, are the following:

(a)—The immediate modification by the National Congress of paragraph 16 of Article 147 of the Federal Constitution, which establishes the requirement of "prior indemnification, just and in cash" for cases of expropriation of lands
in the social interest. This disposition should be eliminated
and replaced by one that would specify that indemnification
for expropriation in the social interest should be made with
long-term, low-interest, non-negotiable government bonds.

(b)—An urgent and complete cadastral survey of all
properties containing more than 500 hectares and of their
use.

(c)—Expropriation by the federal government of the

unused lands in properties of more than 500 hectares, beginning with those in the most densely populated areas, near the great urban centers, along the principal routes of communication, and near the reserves of water.

(d)—Adoption of a plan to provide for the indemnification with long-term, low-interest federal bonds of [the owners of] lands that are expropriated and at values of the lands as these are registered for tax purposes.

(e)—A complete cadastral survey of all public lands by the federal, state, and municipal authorities.

(f)—The re-examination and bringing up to date of all deeds to land, and nullification of illegal or questionable titles to lands that should revert to the public domain.

(g)—A rural land tax that would be progressive, by means of legislation establishing: (1) a heavy increase of the taxes upon the large agricultural estates; and (2) exemption of small farms from taxation.

(h)—Regulation of the sale, concession of right to use, and leasing of lands that are expropriated from the latifundia, taking into account that there can be no concessions of areas containing more than 500 hectares, nor of tracts that are smaller than the minimum necessary to meet the needs of the small rural economic unit.

(i)—Public lands (national, state, and municipal) should be granted gratuitously, except in cases of national interest, to those who wish to cultivate them definitively.

(j)—The delivery of public lands to those who would use them for speculative purposes should be prohibited.

[No k.]

(l)—Titles should be bestowed to those squatters who are effectively working the land, and they should be given increased protection of their rights against those who make a business of falsifying titles to land.

(m)—Nuclei of peasant economies should be planned, facilitated, and stimulated through the formation of production cooperatives.

With a view to the rapid increase of production, especially of food crops, which can meet and correct the stifling cost of living of which the population of the country is complaining, especially the laboring masses in city and country, the government should elaborate a plan for fostering agriculture which would ensure maximal compensatory prices at the sources of production; [ensure] efficient and cheap transportation; favor the purchase of agricultural implements and other aids to production; guarantee supplies of seeds, fertilizers, insecticides, etc., for small farmers; concede available credit to small farmers, whether or not they are farm owners; and combat favoritism to the great *fazendeiros*.

The First National Congress of Farmers and Agricultural Laborers calls upon the Brazilian people to take this banner in its hands and to make it victorious. Belo Horizonte, November 17, 1961.

10

BASES OF THE AGRARIAN REFORM IN BOLIVIA

José Flores Moncayo

❧

Irresponsible persons frequently assert that the agrarian reform decreed August 2, 1953, constitutes a nebulous doctrine whose vague and unprecise principles have no application to concrete realities. Such a depreciative affirmation will not bear the least criticism, and is evidenced by noting that this body of agrarian-indigenistic dispositions conforms adequately to the imperative of social justice whose objective is the solution of the problems of the Indian and those of the land.

As a matter of fact, the bases of Bolivia's agrarian reform may be summarized in accordance with the classical arrangement of the institutes or institutions as follows: the law of juridical and natural persons; the law of property, its forms and functions; legislation pertaining to agrarian matters and agricultural and stockraising activities; and legislation pertaining to labor, individual and in associations.

Translated from José Flores Moncayo, *Derecho Agrario Boliviano* (La Paz: Editorial Don Bosco, 1956), pp. 239-245. Printed by permission of the author.

This arrangement has a definite social orientation which can serve as a basis for future sociological development and advancement.

This is why, in a special manner, the indicated legal disposition No. 03464 postulates and declares:

The original rights of the Bolivian Nation with respect to lands and waters.

The recognition of the persons of the present workers of the land, along with those of other classes of agriculturists, in order to give concrete expression to their rights in the process of the agrarian reform.

The recognition of the right to property based upon its economic and social function.

The juridical rationalization of agricultural and stockraising activities.

The economic and cultural structures of Bolivia's future society.

BOLIVIA'S NATIONAL RIGHTS

Article 1 of Decree-Law No. 03464 states: "The soil, the subsoil, and waters throughout the territory of the Republic belong by original right to the Bolivian Nation." This Article, which we might say proclaims the virtual nationalization of the land in Bolivia, is in harmony, with emphasis upon the land and the water, with the precept contained in Article 108 of the Political Constitution of the State which says: "In addition to the things which the law presently gives this quality, the original dominion of the State includes all portions of the mineral kingdom, all unpatented lands with all their natural riches, the waters of all lakes, rivers, and medicinal springs, as well as all physical forces susceptible of economic use. The laws shall establish the conditions of this dominion as well as those of adjudication to individuals."

It must be noted that in the first of these Articles (Article 1 of Decree-Law No. 03464 of August 2, 1953) the Bolivian Nation is used in place of State to designate the titular person from which the Agrarian Law emanates. This fact, to judge by the comparative legislation on this subject, using the Mexican agrarian reform as an example,[1] concurs in establishing that the Nation, the *National*, is the social primogenitor which has the eminent domain and which is conscious of being organized in order to accomplish its own social and economic objectives. In a similar manner this article assists one in understanding that ownership is subordinated to the public national dominion, since it is a part of the whole: the national territory.

THE JURIDICAL PERSONALITY OF THOSE WHO WORK THE LAND

Another of the bases of the agrarian reform is the juridical recognition of the personality of the man who works the land.

This social and juridical base, incorporated in a positive form in international legislation, is expressed in the new Bolivian Agrarian Law in the principle: "The land belongs to the one who cultivates it."

In reality the incorporation [into the law] of this social and human principle does not merely constitute the proclamation of a new source of proprietary rights, it bestows upon the person, action, and rights of the worker and agricultural and pastoral work all of the attributes of the civil person.

ECONOMIC AND SOCIAL FUNCTION AS ONE CONDITION OF PROPERTY RIGHTS

We have already stated that the classical legal concept of absolute ownership has evolved in modern times to the

---

[1] The first part of Article 27 of the Political Constitution of the United States of Mexico states: "The property rights to the lands and waters included within the limits of national territory pertain originally to the Nation, which has had and has the right to transfer dominion over them to individuals, thus constituting private property."

point that property is no longer an unrestricted teleological factor in the personal riches of an individual; on the contrary, it is an instrument for complementing man's personality in his social life.

This being said, we see that the Bolivian agrarian reform, by postulating that work and the actual possession by the Bolivian country people are the fundamentals of the law of property, has added to the human personality, "because man," as Ossorio y Gallardo says, "just as he needs his own name, personal credit, a family of his own, needs his own private possessions, since these are the stimulus for his work, the premium for his dynamism, the spur to his ingenuity, and the assurance of his future." Indeed, Article 78 of Decree-Law No. 03464[2] establishes and gives positive form to the new source, labor, of property rights.

But this new foundation of proprietary rights lacks sense if we do not consider the worker-proprietor bound to the social body, and to the national production; because the one who has a property is obligated to do everything demanded by the collective interest, in the same way that property always exacts the effective possession of the land and the expenditure of labor in its cultivation.

Effective possession of the land and the application of labor in its cultivation constitute the *sine qua non* of the law of property. But this condition to which is subject the right to use, to enjoy, and to receive the benefits of the land, inherent in the collective interest, is the provision that is established in order to extinguish and leave such rights null

---

[2] Article 78 of Decree-Law No. 03464 reads: "The *campesinos* who have been subjected to feudal regimes of work and exploitation in their conditions of serfs, *obligados, arrimantes, pegujaleros, agregados, forasteros,* etc., who are above the age of eighteen, those above fourteen years of age who are married, and their widows with minor-aged children, are declared to be, with the promulgation of the present Decree, proprietors of the parcels of land which they presently have and work until such time as the National Agrarian Reform Service has given to them, in a rational manner, the lands to which they are entitled in accordance with the definitions of the small farm or compensates them with the collective use of lands that will permit them to cover their family budgets."

and void through the failure to possess and cultivate; that is, the social function of production. One expression of this is contained in Article 77 of Decree-Law No. 03464[3] which establishes the period of two years for the undertaking of agricultural work.

Property so defined, as a social and economic being, has had to structure itself in the new Bolivian Agrarian Law seeking objectives that are complementary in the progressive process of the nation's production. National collective interest intends to give the campesino a house in which to live and to shelter him from the elements with the *campesino's lot;* to secure for the rural family the elevation of its level of living in a way that it may care for its economic and cultural needs with the *small property;* to seek that the *medium property* send to the market the principal part of its production minus that equivalent to the necessities of the agriculturist. The *agricultural enterprise* itself will perform its social function by sustaining the foundation of rural industry.

In complying with an imperative of justice, the Bolivian agrarian reform has disposed that the lands of the community shall be returned to their traditional and institutional owners, establishing that these shall prevail by means of guarantees contained in Articles 57 and 124 of the Agrarian Reform Law. Cooperative property is also reconstituted by the law. The community directed by modern cooperative systems will provide the basis of a progressive agrarian collectivism.

JURIDICAL RATIONALIZATION OF AGRICULTURAL AND STOCKRAISING ACTIVITIES

The panorama of social life in Bolivia presented in the juridical order a disproportionate and antidemocratic exist-

---

[3] Article 77 states: "All Bolivians above eighteen years of age, irrespective of sex, who dedicate or wish to dedicate themselves to agricultural labor shall be given lands where they are available in accordance with the plans of the Government, providing that within the period of two years they undertake agricultural endeavors."

ence of the masses of indigenous campesinos and the minorities privileged before the procedures of the civil and penal Judicial Tribunals. It was a legislation placed at the service of the dominant interests and which discriminated against the Indian in his civil capacity, in his patrimony, and in his acts. The bureaucratic stupor of those enslaved to the dead letter of the codes failed to quench the Indians undying thirst for justice.

The agrarian reform was established with indigenistic and juridical propositions in order to rationalize with justice the rural realities of the country. In this endeavor it had to liberate the Indian from his incapacity (minority and tutelage), extending to him full civil rights, making of him the subject and not the object of law, a person and not a *colono* [agricultural laborer comparable to the *colonus* of late Roman times] subject to sale; it declared him to be the holder of property rights, an owner and not merely an occupant of the land.

The juridical rationalization established by the agrarian reform intends, finally, to establish a democratic regime in Bolivian institutions wherein the rural Indian will have guarantees equal to, and not less than, those of the other classes. In accord with this proposition and with respect to the political rights of the rural Indian, the Decree-Law of July 21, 1952, was promulgated, instituting the right of suffrage (universal right to vote) for the Bolivian campesino.

Relative to labor in agriculture and stockraising, with the agrarian reform have been established the conditions necessary to bring the agricultural laborer, the peon on the estate and, in general, the operator of the farm, under specialized labor legislation. One immediate task of the Agrarian Reform is to complete the Rural Labor Statute.

11

OBJECTIVES OF AGRARIAN REFORM IN BOLIVIA

José Flores Moncayo

In contrast with many countries in which agrarian reforms have been carried on with the objectives of establishing technical agricultural bases for the rational and scientific cultivation of the soil, the Bolivian agrarian reform established its objectives in the dual bases of *indigenism* and *agrarianism*.

Fundamentally, the agrarian reform proposes to elevate the levels of the indigenous [Indian] economy so as to liberate the country from illiteracy, poverty, and fear; and to place within the reach of the Indian the right to property, which will add to the personality of the human being, giving him opportunities to shape his own destiny within the social order.

Above all, the process of rationalization of national life which is set under way by this transformation is justified because it is inconceivable that education alone—as the con-

Translated from José Flores Moncayo, *Derecho Agrario Boliviano* (La Paz: Editorial Don Bosco, 1956), pp. 234-236. Printed by permission of the author.

servatives maintain—could have solved Bolivia's rural problem. It was necessary, therefore, to change the irrational proprietary rights, which were monopolized by a few self-centered and idle hands, and to legislate dominion over the land in favor of the great majority, the agricultural laborers; even more so since historically and juridically it has been demonstrated that the land has always belonged to the native Indians.

The agrarian reform of Ucureña, re-establishing Indian and agrarian measures adapted to national needs, postulated as fundamental objectives: to free the rural people from their servile condition; to stimulate production; to conserve the nation's natural resources; and to promote currents of internal migration. All of this was to preclude any kind of demagogic speculation, so inadequate for Bolivia's historic hour.

As a matter of fact, in Bolivia the socio-economic aspects of rural life were those of the feudalistic-colonial stage, and it was necessary to direct them toward the industrialization of the countryside and the installation of capitalism as a necessary step in the nation's historical development.

[The reform] did not include in any sense the socialization of the land, because the wealth and production of the nation were and remain pitifully low, and misery cannot be socialized.

It was necessary to adjudicate the rights of ownership to the Bolivian *campesinos* because merely to concede them the use of the land would have been to sanction the uncertain and precarious tenancy which was used by the *latifundistas* to destroy their landholding traditions. These and other aspects of the agrarian reform that were put into operation in Bolivia constitute a monumental transformation which will even safeguard Bolivia's existence among the nations of the world.

12

THE PROCESS OF AGRARIAN REFORM IN BOLIVIA

Eduardo Arze-Loureiro

Throughout the history of Bolivia, the social attitudes related to the agrarian problem found expression in accordance with cultural values and the power of each of the social classes. The process involves economic and cultural aspects, social stratification and social mobility, status, power, and rights. Three historical stages may be distinguished: The first is that of the colonial forms which persisted into the period of the Republic, and it was characterized by *latifundismo* and government by a minority; the second stage featured the weakening of the huge landed property through subdivision by inheritance and the sale of tracts to the Indians (and simultaneously, in the cities, socialism, a new factor, was oriented toward the destruction of the colonial order); the third stage is one of government and power in the service of the *campesinos* and the expropriation of the land—this is to say, the realization of the agrarian reform.

Translated from Eduardo Arze-Loureiro, *Actitudes Sociales Relacionadas con la Reforma Agraria en Bolivia*, Mimeographed (Caracas: 1959), pp. 25-32. Printed by permission of the author.

1. From colonial times until the year 1930 a semi-feudal system prevailed, with huge estates of the "white" masters served by the Indian families traditionally established on them. The control of the land was combined with forms of racial submission which prevailed in all aspects of national life. The institutions of the State and the municipality were agencies for the power of the "whites" and "mestizos" over the masses of the Indians. During this lengthy period there was no sign of the disintegration of the latifundium. The two predominant attitudes of the epoch were, on the one hand, the prepotency of the "whites" and "mestizos," and, on the other, the resigned submission of the Indians.

2. The economic crises of the decade 1920-1930 produced in some areas the subdivision of large and middle-sized properties, permitting the Indian to purchase the land that he worked. There developed among the campesinos an interest in saving money for the purpose of purchasing land. A considerable part of the indigenous rural population tended to incorporate into their value systems some elements of the urban culture, such as the language and the modern style of men's dress. In the power relationships and social rights the colonial kind of domination of the other groups over the Indians still persisted. During this epoch the intellectualism of the middle class denounced the condition of social injustice which burdened the Indian.

Following 1930 the experience of the Chaco War, the local organization of the community for the purpose of establishing rural schools by the localities themselves, the diffusion of socialist principles, and the development of agricultural unions produced a clear definition of national attitudes toward the Indian problem and the land problem. The Left proclaimed the slogan, "The Mines to the State, the Land to the People," while the Right used its influence in the governments to contain the new tendency. Simultaneously with the maturing of the new social consciousness, the young generations of Indians more frequently went to the cities as manual laborers, industrial workers, and soldiers, where they learned to read and write and used military service as a means of becoming integrated with other groups. In 1945 the revolutionary nationalist government invited the Indians to take part in a national congress of campesinos, in which it was resolved to abolish certain practices such as the rendering of personal services; these resolutions were converted into governmental decrees and immediately put into effect. In this congress, government officials suggested that the Indians strengthen their organization as one step toward future actions of expropriating the latifundia. Subsequently, in an intermediate period of conservative government, episodes in which the Indians invaded the *haciendas* of the plateau were cruelly repressed. In the "Indian communities" the habitual extortions from the people by the "mestizos" continued.

3. In 1952 and the years that followed, the new revolutionary government nationalized the mines of the large companies, and by all means of communication the leftist politicians, in a campaign of agitation in the rural districts of an intensity previously unknown, exhorted the campesinos to mobilize themselves for the agrarian reform. The indigenous population responded to this call with a mobilization organized by haciendas and districts, and assumed power in the open country by means of the agricultural unions, as a new institution coordinated with the central national power. The large landowners and the "mestizos" of the villages lost all of their class and personal power over the Indians. Travel through the rural districts was no longer fearful for the Indian, but fearful for the "white" and the "mestizo." This new social attitude was expressed in the mentality of the group rather than in that of the individual; the actions were those of the union not those of persons.

[On other pages of the report Dr. Arze described in more detail the actual steps in Bolivia's quick agrarian reform, in paragraphs that are inserted at this point in the résumé which was translated for inclusion in this volume. These paragraphs are as follows:]

The 1952 presidential elections, as a political prism, gave a clear reflection of the social attitudes. The mining companies launched their own candidate, supplied with large sums for the purchase of votes; the bureaucracy and the large landowners named their own, who placed his chances in the possibilities of official pressures throughout the provincial districts; and the opposition gave its support to the platform of the Nationalistic Revolutionary Movement, grouping all of the reform and revolutionary sectors about a standard which emblazoned the basic national problems.

The election results were in favor of the opposition majority. This was the first time in Bolivian history that a situation of this kind had arisen. Then there occurred one of those instances that are so typical of our Latin American politics. The president in power, instead of transferring the command to the successful candidate, chose to deliver the government into the hands of a military junta which tore up the electoral results. This junta was of an immature composition. Personal differences arose among its members to a degree that produced conflict between the armed units which they commanded. In La Paz there was combat between the police brigades and the Army. The latter bombarded the residential districts of the workers. Again the people went into the streets to fight on their own account. Thousands of deaths were counted during the three days of combat within the city. It is important to note how an incident within the military junta set off such a large and widespread popular action. The struggle now was not in terms of persons or of cliques, but in terms of programs; and the victory was that of the people directed by the Nationalistic Revolutionary Movement. With the termination of the fighting, the masses once more spoke freely of their problems. There were neither reprisals nor persecutions, but rejoicing at the ability to deal with the fundamental problems of the nation. The leaders could offer no less than the nationalization of the mines of the large companies and the agrarian reform.

The workers in the mines and factories strengthened their union and its voice predominated in all situations. The pressure was from the bottom to the top; and the fundamental measures for the nationalization of those great companies were merely a response to a burning demand. In contrast, on the agrarian question, the peasants, with their traditional attitude of awaiting governmental orientation, were gradually awakened to the extent that official political propaganda arrived and was disseminated in their communities.

Of the great mass of two million Indians, all the men were called upon to present themselves in the cities to hear the promises of delivering to them the lands on which they had traditionally lived a hopeless existence. This promise was made with full official support.

The indigenous groups of Quechuas and Aymaras, who are distinguished by their traditional integration, surged forth strongly organized by haciendas and localities. The Indian bands from the various localities, with no supplies except parched corn or dehydrated potatoes, flocked into the cities, traveling on foot as many as four days to participate in the huge processions. This awakening of the Indians commenced with the increasing awareness of their great numbers and their high degree of homogeneity. It was a stage in mass indoctrination and, at the same time, a disposition to struggle in the political field in support of the program of land distribution.

. . . . . .

In the era of the agrarian reform, the political movement and the governmental proclamation definitively liquidating the semi-feudal practices were accompanied by an intense agitation, directed systematically from the cities, for the purpose of securing a massive intervention of the campesinos. This time the traditional Indian practice of accepting the mandates of the State was given to the message of total mobilization. Now the State was no longer a repressive force, but a stimulus for the occupation of the land, for the transformation of serf into owner, for the establishment of the campesinos' own local government, and for the definitive elimination of the patronal regime and the extortions by the "mestizos" of the towns. The Indians, who previously had no institutions for the solution of their problems, were given guidance in the organization of agricultural unions identified with their respective localities. It was a rapid action because the social groups were traditionally established in definite ecological areas. Also rapid was the distribution of the land into family parcels and collective fields. With the march to the cities, coordination on departmental and national scales, and the distribution of firearms, the agricultural unions became active and powerful, and they came to constitute the system of power and authority in the rural districts.

With surprising rapidity the land was taken and distributed, without violence, even before the promulgation of the Agrarian Reform Decree. The process took place almost simultaneously throughout the vast zone which is inhabited by 80 per cent of the national population, and this with all its amplitude and with a stability that precluded the necessity for subsequent revisions. The rapid and organic change was based upon the great predominance of the previous feudal organization in which specific and delimited tracts of ground were assigned for the use of each family, and, at the same time, norms were established for the participation of each family in the collective work for the master. This is to say that the land was already divided, the work organized, and the patterns established, none of which has been altered, except the juridical basis, with the passing of the property rights from the hands of the large landowner to those of the social group traditionally established on the hacienda. It has been a peaceful process, although one of transcendent importance, because it has eliminated one rural social class, that of the latifundistas, and has converted the serf into the owner of his parcel and a member of an institution with common possessions and interests.

The enormous disproportion between campesinos and large landowners, and the decision of the agricultural unions to fight, induced the large landowners to retreat to the cities. Deprived of their personal power on the haciendas, and with the local police systems replaced by union guards, in the country they were left without possibility for direct action. As a result they oriented themselves toward the recuperation of their power in the State. Lacking any support from the masses, they decided to dedicate themselves to the typical way of securing power in Bolivia: the *coup d'état*.

The withdrawal of the "whites" from the Andean countryside was simultaneous with the occupation of the land by the Indians. This was an epoch of group attitudes as a part of the political program of the revolutionary government, and of the exclusion of the large landowners. Although the Agrarian Reform Decree was dictated, the events were produced without taking it into account, except solely in those aspects that were favorable to the agricultural unions. Within each union the seizure of the land took place with order and understanding, although as time passed some evidences of the prepotency of the union leaders appeared. The existing subdivision of use in the feudal organization served as the basis for appropriation merely by the simple process of adding to the [campesino] families' right of occupancy.

13

THE COMMUNISTS' TACTICS
RELATIVE TO AGRARIAN
REFORM IN CHILE
Luis Corvalan

Since September 4, 1958, much has been said in our country about the awakening *campesino*. This is entirely justified. The large vote which the people's candidate received in the agricultural provinces was not a simple and temporary act of rebellion. It marked the swing of the countryside to the Left, and it put into effect the alliance between workers and campesinos on a scale that had previously only been dreamed about.

For many the large leftist vote in the rural districts constituted a surprise or a fact determined by the change from the old system of voting to that of the single ballot. The truth is that it represents an absolutely logical phenomenon in which the decisive element was not the introduction of a new system of suffrage. Despite the facts that the domination of the great landowners constituted a strong drawback and that agricultural production was falling steadily, the Chilean countryside could not remain perfectly un-

Translated from Luis Corvalan, *Cosas Nuevas en el Campo* (Santiago: Imprenta Lautaro, 1960 [?]), pp. 3-22.

changeable in any sense. The advance of the means of communication, the development of crops for industrial purposes, the mechanization of agricultural activities, although
all on a small scale, and above all the great events of our
epoch, have led to a certain change in the mentality of the
campesino.

The political and cultural ties between the city and the
country, between the proletariat and the campesinos, have
developed in many ways. The children of campesinos who
go to work in industry learn many things which they soon
teach to their relatives and friends who have remained on
the *hacienda* or in the village and with whom they maintain contacts. Thousands of *inquilinos* [one of the types of
resident workers on the haciendas] and small owners have
become laborers in the construction of hydroelectric plants,
roads, reservoirs, and canals, or have been incorporated into
the infant industries of sugar or lumber, and live alongside
numerous members of the proletariat who come from the
cities. Furthermore, the crisis and the repressive measures
employed against the urban laboring class have caused many
of the workers in the mines and factories to return to the
country. Throughout Chile, on the haciendas and in the villages, we have seen many laborers, including some who were
union leaders in the nitrate, coal, and copper [industries].
It follows that the political work of the popular parties, and
especially of us Communists, should also figure among the
principal elements that have influenced and are influencing
the creation of a new social conscience in the countryside.

MORE STRUGGLE AND ORGANIZATION

Contrary to what may be believed, the campesinos have
not crossed their arms nor are they merely awaiting future
electoral battles. Whoever believes that there is dead calm in
the country is mistaken. In one way or another the campesinos defend themselves from exploitation by the great landowners and fight for their rights. They do it as they can,
even coming to the desperate and individual use of firearms, as in the cases of Gregorio Escobar, a laborer at Ani-

huarraque, and many Indians to the south of the Bío-Bío. Thousands of "volunteers" who refuse to work for the lowest wages, and go from one *fundo* [large estate] to another to hire out where the pay is best, provoke a certain scarcity of labor at harvest time. More and more they are using their work to obtain a larger income, even though this may involve long and exhausting journeys. Thousands of rural workers call upon their employers and the authorities for the payment of family allowances, minimum wages, a fixed number of hours of work per week, and the provision of social security, of which the large landowners make a mockery.

From these and other elementary ways of defending their rights in some places the campesinos pass to more advanced forms, to organization and organized struggle. As yet they do not follow this route on a large scale; but the important thing is to make a beginning. New organizations of the campesinos have arisen at the same time that the existing ones have been strengthened. [. . .]

The number of lawsuits and petitions, and of work stoppages and strikes, that have arisen recently in the rural districts are also relatively important. [. . .]

FEAR IS DISAPPEARING

These facts reveal that the campesinos are losing their fear and acquiring self-confidence. This is very important. The sentiment of fear favors oppression by the large landowners and should be considered as the worst ill and the most serious obstacle that hinders the organization and struggle of the campesinos. For this reason it is necessary to promote the loss of fear. The large landowners, and not the campesinos, should be fearful. The campesinos are most numerous. The agricultural laborers and inquilinos number more than half a million rural workers, who with the members of their families and the families of others in the modest social strata total more than two million persons. Furthermore, they fight in a just cause. The large landowners are few, not exceeding 2,000, and they are destined to disappear historically. If the affairs of the large landowners are

examined carefully, [it is evident that] they fear the campesinos much more than the latter fear them. The great rich
ones of the rural districts have not slept well since they
learned the results of September 4, and especially since the
triumph of the Cuban Revolution with the decisive support
of the campesinos and the beginning in Cuba of giving
reality to the slogan, "the land is for those who work it."
The large landowners fear rebellion by the campesinos more
than they do fire or the devil. [. . .]

SINGLE AND INDEPENDENT UNIONS

With respect to organization, it is necessary to take a flexible position, as is required by the complex conditions of the
countryside. The important thing is to organize in any
form, in legal or in independent unions, in simple commit-
tees of campesinos, in cooperatives, and even in cultural and
sports centers. In some places the groups should consist
solely of agricultural laborers and inquilinos, in others solely
of small proprietors and other non-proletarian groups, and in
other places of all the sectors, from the agricultural laborers
to the small and middle-sized farmers. The forms of organization should be in accord with the wishes of the campesinos themselves; but we Communists believe that the
best form of organization is that of the independent union,
with headquarters in the village, in which are grouped the
workers from various fundos and all of the modest sectors of
the rural population from the wage hand to the small proprietor, including the sharecropper, the poor campesino, etc.
There are more disadvantages than advantages connected
with the organization into legal unions. [. . .]

VARIED METHODS OF FIGHTING

With respect to the methods of carrying on the fight in
the countryside, it is also necessary to take a flexible position, in accordance with the conditions in each locality.
There are places where the objective and subjective conditions permit an open fight. In other places it is different;

there still is fear, lack of confidence, etc. In the localities where there are the most difficulties, and this fear and lack of confidence exist, the beginning should be as simple as possible: a denouncement of the abuses in our press and before the public tribunal and a protest to the authorities without revealing the names of the campesinos who have supplied the information.

It is also desirable to know well how to select the time for beginning and carrying on the struggle with the greatest probabilities of success. There is no doubt that in general the best time is in the harvest period, when the fear of a stoppage, a delay of two or three days, makes the large landowner tremble.

Likewise, it is necessary to know whom to support to the greatest degree. Of all the rural sectors the agricultural laborers are, naturally, the most determined, especially the volunteers, those from the outside, who receive their payment in cash, have no other ties to the hacienda, and work only irregularly. [. . .]

The inquilino, because he is a semi-proletarian, because he is bound to the hacienda by the dwelling and the piece of ground he is permitted to use, and because of other favors, is not as combative as the agricultural laborer properly designated. But he has the advantage over the latter of being more steadily employed, so it is advisable to consider him useful and to have him present for the defense of the gains that are made, for the continuity of the struggle, and for the solidity of the organizations. [. . .]

TENDER A HAND TO THE COUNTRYSIDE

The conditions under which the rural population live are truly miserable. The minimum wage [is extremely low]. The agricultural laborer has no retirement, no indemnity for years of service, no right to vacations. The inquilino is charged up to 75 per cent of his wage for gifts. The breadstuffs, the peas, and the piece of land (which generally does not exceed half a *cuadra* and frequently is one fourth of a *cuadra*) [he is allowed] are insufficient to offset the "lacks" he cannot acquire with what he receives in cash. Even without taking into account the mockery of the minimum wage by the landowners, their stealing of the family allotments, and their other abuses, it may be asserted that the situation of the rural laborers is truly pitiful. Their clothing gets progressively poorer. The use of sandals is increasing. The diet is poor and inadequate. Many rural workers go entire days with no food except toasted flour with water, a *tortilla* with a pepper, salt, and sometimes an onion. The little poultry they can raise is not to eat but to sell in order to purchase lard, salt, and sugar in the village.

The position of those in the other lowly rural strata is not substantially better. Many small owners have so little land that it will not satisfy their needs during the year. Credit and aid from the State does not reach them; these are monopolized by the great *latifundistas*. They cry out when it rains heavily or when it rains little, obtain the support of the banks, and leave nothing for the poor. Under these circumstances, many small landowners become agricultural laborers or join the construction crews of reservoirs, canals, and roads. [. . .]

OLD THEORIES AND NEW POSSIBILITIES

It is also necessary to emphasize that the worsening of the agricultural crisis makes agrarian reform all the more imperative. It was not by accident that the latest convention of the Conservatives spoke of this problem, that the Liberal Party engaged in a week of study of agricultural matters, that the Radical Party is presenting an agrarian reform project, that this was one of the central themes of the Summer School at the University of Chile, that President Alessandri has named a committee on the reorganization of agriculture, and finally that a host of articles on this problem are appearing in *El Mercurio, El Diario Ilustrado,* and *La Nación*. They are merely toying with this all-important subject. They want to make an agrarian reform of words to prevent one in reality. Under the guise of agrarian reform, they wish to get control of the State lands. But if they see that they must become demagogic in this matter, it is because the solution for this problem cannot wait and they wish to avoid having the people, and especially the campesinos, take it into their own hands and solve it in their own way.

The giving of the land to those who work it has become the greatest aspiration of the campesinos. For its fulfillment we should mobilize and organize forces, principally in the rural districts, planting the problem not only in general terms but also in concrete forms, giving principal attention to the places in which the government and the reactionaries want things to continue as they have been until now, this is to say in the great latifundia of the central zone, of the South, and of Norte Chico. In each province four or five estates should be selected for a beginning in giving the land to the campesinos who work on them.

We Communists can be proud of having contributed more than anyone else to the awakening of the countryside from the times of our great comrade Rescabarren. We are happy, but in no way satisfied, to count among our numbers some thousands of the rural workers. No less than 20 per cent of our fighters are campesinos; in the agricultural provinces this percentage rises to around 50. All of this is of great value, but it is only a good beginning of a great work in the countryside.

14

AGRARIAN REFORM IN CUBA AS PRESENTED OFFICIALLY

The Council of Ministers, Republic of Cuba

❧

DR. MANUEL URRUTIA LLEO, President of the Republic of Cuba

WHEREIN: The Council of Ministers has approved and I have sanctioned the following:

WHEREAS: The progress of Cuba involves both the growth and diversification of industry in order to facilitate the most effective utilization of its natural resources, by its citizens as well as the elimination of dependence on the one-crop system of agriculture, which still basically persists and is one of the symptoms of our inadequate economic development;

AND WHEREAS: To those ends the Revolutionary Government proposes to pass laws that will safeguard and stimulate private industry by means of protective tariffs, fiscal policies, and the sound handling of public and private credit

Reprinted from Council of Ministers, Republic of Cuba, *Land Reform Law* (Havana: COP, 1960 [?]), pp. 3-14. (This is the official English translation of the law promulgated from the Sierra Maestra, May 17, 1959.)

as well as other forms of industrial development, and at the same time guide Cuban agriculture on the road to essential development and progress;

AND WHEREAS: In all the studies that have been made for the purpose of promoting economic development, especially those undertaken by the United Nations, special attention has been given to the importance of carrying out an Agrarian Reform, insofar as economic matters are concerned with two main goals: (a) to facilitate and increase the growing of new crops to provide the nation's industries with raw materials and to meet food consumption requirements; to develop and expand those items of agricultural production intended for export, a source of foreign exchange for essential imports; and (b) at the same time, to increase the consumer market by means of progressive improvements in the standard of living of those people in the rural areas, which in turn will contribute, by expanding the domestic market, toward the establishment of industries that are not very profitable in a limited market and to develop other lines of products that are limited for the same reason;

AND WHEREAS: According to the opinion repeatedly expressed by the technical experts, in the case of Cuba the goals set forth in the preceding clause are attainable and, as an additional stimulus for those necessary changes in the present agrarian set-up in our country, it has become urgently necessary to rescue the great majority of the rural population of Cuba from the state of poverty in which it has traditionally struggled;

AND WHEREAS: In Cuban agriculture frequent use is made of the sharecropping agreement and of the system of ground rents, which discourage the farmer by placing inequitable, uneconomical, and in many cases extortionary obligations upon him, thus preventing the best utilization of the land;

AND WHEREAS: The National Agricultural Census of 1946 showed that the great majority of the farms now being cultivated are being worked by persons who do not own the land and who work it as sharecroppers, tenant farmers (including sugar-cane growers), and squatters, while the ownership rights are vested in absentee landlords, which in many cases constitutes a social injustice and in all cases represents a factor that discourages productive efficiency;

AND WHEREAS: In the said Agricultural Census the extreme and undesirable concentration of land ownership in a few hands also became evident, and it was found that 2,335 farms represent ownership of an area of 317,000 *caballerías*[1] of land, which means that 1.5 percent of the owners possess more than 46 percent of all the farm land of the country, a situation that is still more serious if it is kept in mind that some owners possess several very large farms;

AND WHEREAS: In contrast to the situation described in the foregoing clause, we have the phenomenon of 111,000 farms of less than two *caballerías* each, which comprise an area of only 76,000 *caballerías*, which in turn means that seventy percent of the farms occupy less than twelve percent of the nation's farm land and in addition there is a large number of farms, about 62,000, that occupy an area of less than three fourths of a *caballería* each;

AND WHEREAS: It is obvious that in large farms there is a detrimental failure to utilize the natural resources, the soil, the cultivated areas being used in ways that produce a low yield, and too much space being devoted to large-scale cattle raising, and other areas that could be reclaimed for productive activities being left completely fallow and in some cases covered with *marabú* bushes;

AND WHEREAS: It is unanimously agreed that the existence of large landholdings, as shown by the foregoing data, not only runs counter to the modern concept of social justice but constitutes one of the factors that shape the underdeveloped, dependent structure of the Cuban economy, as can be demonstrated by pointing out various characteristics, among which are the following: the fact that the national income depends on production for export, considered the "strategic variable" of the Cuban economy, which is thus highly vulnerable to the cyclican depressions of the world

---

[1] The *caballería* is about 33 acres. [Translator's note]

economy; the strong propensity to import, including goods that under other conditions could be produced in Cuba; the consequent lessening of opportunity for profit from local investments and the reduction in our own exports; the technical backwardness of the methods of cultivation and of operating the cattle industry; in general, the low standard of living of the Cuban people and in particular of the rural population, with the consequent low purchasing power to the domestic market, which is unable, under such conditions, to encourage the development of national industry;

AND WHEREAS: The Constitution of 1940 and the Organic Law of the Revolutionary Government prohibits large landholdings and provides that measures to abolish them permanently shall be provided by law;

AND WHEREAS: The constitutional provisions in force provide that private property may be expropriated by the State, provided it is established that such expropriation is in the public interest;

AND WHEREAS: It is preferable to replace the production from large landholding, which is uneconomical and based on extensive cultivation, by cooperative production, based on intensive cultivation and the use of technical methods, which brings with it the advantages of large-scale production;

AND WHEREAS: It is essential to establish a technical body that can apply and carry out in every detail the aims of economic development, with the resulting improvement in the standard of living for the Cuban people, in accordance with the letter and the spirit of this law;

AND WHEREAS: It is advisable to take measures to prevent the future alienation of Cuban Land to foreigners, while at the same time we hereby attest our remembrance and admiration of the patrician figure of Manuel Sanguily, the first Cuban who, as early as 1903, foresaw the terrible consequences of large landholdings and introduced a bill in the Congress of our Republic to prevent the control of Cuban resources by foreigners;

Therefore: In exercise of the powers vested in it by the

Organic Law of the Republic, the Council of Ministers resolves to enact the following law to be known as the

AGRARIAN REFORM LAW OF THE REPUBLIC OF CUBA

CHAPTER I

Land in General

ARTICLE 1. Large landholding is hereby prohibited. The maximum area of land that a natural or juridical person may own shall be thirty *caballerías*. Land owned by a natural or juridical person in excess of that limit will be expropriated for distribution among the peasants and agricultural workers who have no land. [. . .]

ARTICLE 3. The land of the State, the provinces, and the municipalities shall also be subject to distribution. [. . .]

ARTICLE 5. The order of priority in each Agrarian Development Zone, for expropriation, when necessary, and for the redistribution of land shall be as follows:

(a) The lands of the State and those privately owned lands on which farmers are established as tenants, subtenants, tenants growing sugar cane, subtenants growing sugar cane, sharecroppers, and squatters;

(b) The excess areas of lands not protected by the exemptions contained in Article 2 of this Law;

(c) All other lands that may become subject [to this Law]. [. . .]

ARTICLE 6. Privately owned lands up to a limit of thirty *caballerías* per person or entity shall not be subject to expropriation unless affected by contracts with tenant farmers who grow sugar cane, subtenant farmers who grow sugar cane, tenant farmers, subtenant farmers, and sharecroppers, or occupied by squatters, who hold parcels not larger than five *caballerías* in which case they also shall be subject to expropriation pursuant to the provisions of this Law.

ARTICLE 7. The owners of lands subject to this Law, once the expropriations, grants, and sales to tenant farmers, subtenant farmer [sic], tenant farmers who grow sugar cane, subtenant farmers who grow sugar cane, and squatters established on the farm have been made, may retain the remainder of the property in so far as it does not exceed the maximum area authorized by the Law. [. . .]

ARTICLE 12. Beginning one year after the promulgation of the present Law, corporations may not operate sugar plantations if they fail to meet the following requirements:

(a) That all shares of stock shall be registered;
(b) That the holders of those shares shall be Cuban citizens;
(c) That the holders of those shares shall not be persons who appear as owners, stockholders, or officers of companies engaged in the manufacture of sugar.

After the aforementioned time limit, lands owned by corporations that do not meet the foregoing requisites may be exprop[r]iated for the purposes established in the present Law. Likewise the said corporations shall forfeit their right to such grinding quotas as they may have had when this Law was promulgated.

ARTICLE 13. Nor may natural persons who are owners, stockholders, or officers of corporations engaged in the manufacture of sugar operate sugar plantations. The lands belonging to such persons operating sugar plantations may be exprop[r]iated for the purposes established in the present Law. [. . .]

ARTICLE 15. Rural property may in the future be acquired only by Cuban citizens or companies formed by Cuban citizens.

Farms not larger than thirty *caballerías* which, in the judgment of the National Agrarian Reform Institute, are suitable for conveyance to foreign companies or entities for industrial or agricultural development considered beneficial to the development of the national economy are exempt from the foregoing provision.

In cases of hereditary conveyances of rural properties to heirs who are not Cuban citizens, such properties shall be considered to be subject to expropriation for purposes of the Agrarian Reform, regardless of their size.

CHAPTER II

*Redistribution of Lands and Indemnification
of the Owners*

ARTICLE 16. An area of two *caballerías* for fertile land, without irrigation, distant from urban centers, and devoted to crops of medium economic yield shall be established as a "vital minimum" for a peasant family of five persons.

The National Agrarian Reform Institute shall be the agency charged with establishing and deciding in each case what the necessary "vital minimum" is, starting from the aforesaid base and taking into consideration the average level of annual income it is hoped to attain for each family.

The lands that make up the "vital minimum" shall enjoy the benefits of not being subject to attachment or transfer as referred to in Article 91 of the Organic Law of the Republic.

ARTICLE 17. Private lands subject to exprop[r]iation under the provisions of this Law and lands of the State shall be transferred undivided to the cooperatives recognized by this Law or distributed among the beneficiaries in parcels no larger than two *caballerías*, without prejudice to the adjustments that the National Agrarian Reform Institute may make in order to determine the "vital minimum" in each case. [. . .]

ARTICLE 19. Owners of parcels of land smaller in area than the "vital minimum," who cultivate them personally, shall also be awarded free of charge the land necessary to complete it, provided it is available and the economic and social conditions of the region so permit. [. . .]

ARTICLE 22. The lands that are available for distribution shall, in accordance with the provisions of this Law, be distributed in the following order of priority:

(a) Farmers who have been dispossessed of the land they were cultivating;

(b) Farmers residing in the region where the lands to be distributed are located, who lack land or who cultivate only an area less than the "vital minimum";

(c) Agricultural workers who habitually work and reside on the lands to be distributed;

(d) Farmers of other regions, who lack land or who have an area less than the "vital minimum," preference being given to those of neigboring regions;

(e) Agricultural workers of other regions, preference being given to those of neighboring regions;

(f) Any other person who makes proper application, preference being given to applicants who show that they have knowledge of agricultural matters.

ARTICLE 23. Within the groups mentioned in the preceding article the following shall be given preference:

(a) Veterans of the Rebel Army or dependent members of their families;

(b) Members of the auxiliary corps of the Rebel Army;

(c) Victims of the war or the repression of the tyranny;

(d) Dependent members of the families of persons who have died as a consequence of their participation in the revolutionary struggle against tyranny.

In all cases, heads of families shall have priority. [. . .]

15

THE MEXICAN AGRARIAN REFORM: BACKGROUNDS, ACCOMPLISHMENTS, AND PROBLEMS

Ramón Fernández y Fernández

Was an agrarian reform necessary in Mexico? It is known that one should never use an unconditional "yes" in speaking of historical events; but one cannot resist the temptation to ask: had there been no agrarian reform in Mexico, would the country's agricultural and general economic development have been slower or would it have been more rapid?

It is not easy to answer this question in a simple and conclusive manner. It is necessary to examine the conditions that prevailed in Mexico during the first decade of this century and to see if there was a defective system of land tenure which could be considered as making an agrarian reform necessary or advisable. Naturally, and above all in relation to its first stages, the enemies of the Mexican agrarian reform have denied its necessity and considered it ill-advised and destructive. Nevertheless, little by little the

Translated from Ramón Fernández y Fernández, "La Reforma Agraria Mexicana: Logros y Problemas Derivados," *Boletín de Estudios Especiales* (México), VIII, no. 93 (July, 1957), 211-220. Printed by permission of the author.

idea has spread and is now general throughout my country that the agrarian reform was necessary, and, in addition, that it was a progressive step, with important repercussions in economic development. But these ideas, irrespective of how generally they are found, should not be accepted without analysis. Prudence reminds one to remember that the history was written by those who won.

During the first decade of the century, that is, during the last stage of what is known in Mexican history as the *Porfiriato* (the administration of General Porfirio Díaz), the country undoubtedly made progress; but in the closing years of the decade, clear signs appeared of stagnation and lack of popular support. At this time landownership was highly concentrated in the hands of a few. Agriculture languished, perhaps, along with other reasons, because of the failure to open to cultivation the areas of greatest potentiality, but that required huge investments and regional planning. The government did not undertake this, probably because the prevailing regime of property in land caused this to be left to private initiative, a matter to which the prevailing liberal ideas also contributed. In the year 1909, in order to assist such private initiative in these purposes (and it could be interpreted as an official recognition of the problem that had arisen), the government of General Díaz established the Caja de Préstamos para Obras de Irrigación y Fomento de la Agricultura [Loan Bank for Irrigation Works and the Promotion of Agriculture]. After years of poor harvests, during this year of 1909 a hard freeze struck the plateau and destroyed the crops; this threw into bold relief the debility of the rural sector of the economy. This agricultural disaster contributed to the fall of the regime. Another symptom of the weakness of the agricultural structure was the frequency with which the *haciendas* were mortgaged. In its efforts to enlarge, or perhaps because of the excessive concentration of landownership, the Mexican hacienda had reached a crisis. [. . .]

The social aspects of the situation were also of great importance. The owners of the land, that is the large *hacendados*, despite the frequency with which they were involved in financial difficulties because of the low productivity of their haciendas, were in undisputed possession of the economic power. At the same time they held in their hands the political power. They constituted a landowning aristocracy, accompanied by all of the ill effects that have arisen throughout the history of civilization from the predominance of such a group. Often they were absentees; their estates were left in the hands of administrators, who frequently were inefficient, while they themselves led a life of ostentation, in accordance with what they considered to be the social requirements, in Mexico City or abroad.

An emerging middle class struggled to develop non-agricultural enterprises, industrial, commercial, and financial. Its members were dismayed to find their projects or businesses stifled by the power of the ruling group, which distributed all of the concessions and sought to monopolize all businesses, without being able to supply any genuine stimulation. [The middle class people] were tired of the continued power of the dictator, already aged and surrounded by the same group of favorites. The Revolution burst forth among this progressive middle class, accompanied from the first by some of the elements of rural origin; later, about 1914, it developed the definite aspects of a violent popular uprising in which most of the fighters were *campesinos* who demanded above everything else reforms of an agrarian nature.

In order to understand the situation it is necessary to examine the internal structure of the haciendas. Each of them was a vast territorial seignioralty, tending to be a closed economy because as far as possible the attempt was made to produce on the estate everything needed on it.

The endeavor was made to obtain a secure income from the hacienda, although this was low in relation to the amount of land involved. In order to prevent the flow of money from the estate, scrip or due bills were issued, a kind of special currency of value only on the hacienda and usable only for the purchase of supplies at *la tienda de raya* [or commissary]. Frequently the wages themselves were paid in this scrip. The ideal of a good administration was to get back for the hacienda's coffers the amount that was paid in wages.

The high death rate, the construction of the railroads, and the migration of Mexican workers to the United States were responsible for a chronic labor shortage. As a result the hacienda was confronted with the problem of a rising wage scale. Because the agricultural techniques generally were backward, the returns from the estate did not permit the payment of high wages, and ways were sought to guarantee the labor supply and impede the rise in costs. One of these ways, a very old one, consisted of assigning to each of the regular wage hands (or *acasillados*) a small piece of land (the *pegujal* or *acuaro*) for his own use and as a supplement to his wages. This strengthened the subsistence sector of agriculture, in which the methods were manual and antiquated and the products were not intended for the market. Thus part of the wages were paid in kind with the products of the estate.

Another device for retaining the labor supply, and, because of its social implications and the discontent it produced, even worse than the one just mentioned, was the semi-enslavement of the peons. This was accomplished by means of the old device of debt bondage which had been in use from colonial times. When the worker needed extra funds (because of a marriage, the birth of a child, sickness, or a death in the family), he was given a loan. This he was never able to repay because of the demands upon his wages; but, of great importance to the hacendado, such debts served to reduce the mobility of the workers. The peon who was indebted could not leave the hacienda until after the debt had been paid. If he fled he was pursued as a thief by the rural police. The police returned him to the hacienda, where frequently he was punished by imprisonment in his own cell or even corporally, after which he was returned to work. When through mutual agreement one hacienda transferred laborers to another, the second agreed to assume the laborers' debts to the first, and this came to be nothing more nor less than a sale of slaves. Social services and educational facilities for the workers were conspicuous by their absence, indicative of the hacendados' interest in maintaining the peons in ignorance. The indebted peons came to constitute a separate caste.

The most profitable and secure crops were grown through the use of permanent wage hands, supplemented by temporary workers whose numbers were held to the minimum. The more risky and least profitable crops were left in charge of sharecroppers and tenants.

In spite of all, not everything was dark in life on the haciendas. A certain paternalism in the treatment of the peons occasionally alleviated their misery. Not always was the absence of investment a characteristic of the latifundium: there were haciendas on which considerable improvements were made, such as the construction of irrigation canals, the purchase of machinery, and the introduction of seeds from other countries. The hacienda had a good period at the close of the nineteenth century. But the picture given is a true reflection of the general situation about 1910. The government not only permitted, but actually fostered, the excessive enlargements, and it did nothing to impede the unlimited oppression of the workers.

In the face of this oppression, the laborer turned his eyes to the past. It is human to idealize bygone days, and to attribute virtues to them which are less common in the present. The villages had held their own lands, or the campesinos had possessed their own farms, in accordance with the two types of property rights to the land that had prevailed in Mexico from the times of the Aztecs. The hacienda, in order to grow, had despoiled the villages of their communal holdings, and they had also absorbed the small family-sized farms. It was natural for the campesinos to think that, by recovering the possession of their lost lands, whether communal or private property, they would remedy the bad conditions that prevailed. When large masses of the peasants are deprived of the possession of land and factors prevail which magnify their ancestral anxiety for these rights, an agrarian problem has arisen. The landowning aristocracy of Mexico could not and would not play the reform role that those of other countries have assumed, which could have

prevented the unquestionable evils of a violent social uprising such as occurred in Mexico. The agrarian reform was a
part of this explosion. [. . .]

I believe that enough has been said to indicate that in
Mexico an agrarian reform was necessary, and that the reform itself was a progressive step, even though it was a part
of a revolution and not an evolution. Naturally it gave a
new sense of dignity and liberty to the great and, if you
wish, poorly oriented masses; it aroused many aspirations
and awakened the enterprising spirit of many people. It
transferred hosts of the population from one place to another, and it promoted trade. It channelized large amounts
of available private capital into non-agricultural enterprises,
from which it had fled in the early stages; and this seems to
have made for the diversification of the economy. It influenced the State (and surely this is one of the things that is
most important for agricultural development) to assist
agriculture through the construction of irrigation works, the
establishment of an agricultural credit system, and the
construction of many good roads and trails. Its violence and
confiscatory character may be lamented, but it had, as has
been said, positive effects, direct and indirect, and perhaps
the latter were as important or even more important than
the former. It constitutes a lesson: that reform, when
necessary, should be made before an uprising takes place.
The Mexican agrarian reform, on the contrary, was the result of an uprising, that is to say, it took place under the
most unfavorable conditions. [. . .]

REFORM METHODS

As yet we have not discussed the methods used in the
Mexican agrarian reform. Before describing them, however, it is advisable to emphasize the most important fact
related to these methods. In Mexico agrarian reform was
not a pacific undertaking, nor was it a policy planned for the
solution of economic problems. It lacked not only the con-

tributions of intellectuals to point out the best paths to follow, but one may indicate that among the politicians who directed its first stages there was never any intention of doing what later was done. As a result one may say that the reform was accomplished amid conditions of violence and political animosity, frequently among those with guns in hand, and in the midst of chaos and bloodshed. The first allotments of land were made before there was any corresponding legislation and they came to be known by the significant designation "military possessions." Later these were given legal sanction. The hacendados took up arms for protection and their warring retainers were given the name "white guards." The agrarians long had both plow and rifle, and their extremely bloody military activities were called "agrarian defenses." The country burned in the convulsions of a civil war between multiple factions. Agrarian reform was the way of returning to the promotion of peace.

The Mexican agrarian reform established its course and acquired its impetus in the pursuit of a restitution of land and the ends of social justice, and in accord with the political necessities of the opposing factions: but it was never planned in terms of improving the system of land tenure to make it more favorable to agricultural progress. For this reason it is not strange that there were serious defects in the methods used.

In the first stage, for which the most important document is the discourse of Luis Cabrera in the House of Deputies in 1912, an extremely moderate reform was proposed, so moderate that if this scheme had prevailed its accomplishments would have been inconsequential and doubtless even contrary to the interests of agricultural development. The original or primitive concept of reform assumed that the hacienda would not disappear and that it would have to give up certain lands to the villages, so that each of the agricultural laborers, without ceasing to be a laborer, would have a small tract of his own to cultivate in order to supplement his wages and to cause him to feel more independent. It sought only the legislating of the pegujal or acuaro, which already existed *de facto* on the same haciendas. Simultaneously, the idea was born, which subsequently gained much force, of the restitution of the communal lands to the villages from which they had been taken by the usurpation of the haciendas.

The fundamental concepts which were to serve as the mechanisms of the reform came into Mexican jurisprudence in a Law of January 6, 1915, promulgated in Vera Cruz in a period of full armed conflict. This law was later incorporated in the Constitution of 1917. These concepts may be summarized as follows: the village was established as a primary object of agrarian law; land was restored to or granted to the villages as a permanent and inalienable possession; and the village, in turn, distributed the arable portions of this land among the individuals with rights to it and reserved the pastures and woodlands for community uses and benefit. The residents of the villages who had certain characteristics were those with rights to the land, and the area to be given to a village was calculated in accordance with their number.

A very important feature of the foregoing is the absence of one of the elements that should be present in every well done agrarian reform: the selection of the beneficiaries. In other words, the reform was unleashed on the basis of the creation of a "right to the land" on the part of all campesinos. The right thus generated was bound to be illusory, and carried to its extreme it implied the equal distribution of the whole agricultural area among the entire population dedicated to agriculture, which, despite its equality, no one would defend as the ideal agrarian structure. On the other hand, the reform could not have been unleashed had it involved a more logical process for correcting the defects of the agrarian structure in each region. According to the criterion employed land was distributed to the people, whereas the opposite would have been available following the elaboration of certain means of acquisition or expropriation with corrections as the indicated goals.

To be affected an estate had to be situated within a radius of 7 kilometers of the village asking for land and it had to have an area greater than that considered as exempt. Thus not all of an hacienda was affected, but only the area in excess of that exempted. The part to be retained was designated by the proprietor, so that the best lands tended to remain in private hands. As a result the lands granted to a village were taken from various haciendas, so that frequently the *ejidos* were composed of many widely dispersed tracts. On the other hand the divisions of the estates were made in accordance with no rational plan, divisions of units which, even though ordinarily excessively large, surely had been following throughout the centuries some logical principles of integration, such as the grouping of certain types of soil and a diversity of complementary resources. Likewise no account was taken of the extent to which the hacienda affected was well cultivated or poorly used, of whether it was an extensive tract of land in its natural state or a large capitalistic enterprise, or if it was used directly or indirectly.

From the standpoint of the ejido, the methods used led to the creation of a large number of *minifundia*. For many years the area assigned for the computation of the amount of land to be granted was very small, because the idea of the ejido-pegujal lived on; even when there was insufficient land for distribution it nevertheless was divided among all those with rights to allotments. Moreover, as a result of the reform, there was a proliferation of the number of individual owners with holdings so small that they could not participate in many features of agricultural progress and who had to carry on without technical and economic assistance. Thus subsistence farming was promoted.

The agrarian struggle along the lines described brought about a great waste of the wealth that had been produced by many generations. This wealth was not merely redistributed, but to considerable extent it was lost. The walls of the great haciendas, with their solid construction and great installations, frequently were left vacant and unused. Much irrigated land reverted to dry farming. Forests and perennials disappeared. [. . .] It is possible that the reform in its most active stages brought about a decrease in production, and the statistics seem to support this idea, although not conclusively, because data for 1908 to 1924 are lacking and because there are serious doubts about the data that are available. From 1940 on, however, agricultural production gained impetus and increased rapidly. [. . .]

THE RISE OF A DEMAND FOR REVISIONS

Preoccupations soon arose among those in power in the regime emanating from the Revolution, that is among the authors and promoters of the reform. The old agrarians, the true fathers of the movement, displaced from power by that ungrateful law which says that revolutions devour their children, became bitter critics of what was taking place; they considered that the original principles were being cast aside. The revolutionaries in power frequently were agrarians because of political convenience, and they lacked deep and firm convictions. Until 1934 repeated attempts were made to reduce the speed of or even to terminate the distribution of land. Means were sought (the "ejido districts," for example) to exclude reform of any type from the richest and best-cultivated regions. But it was found that it was politically impossible to detain or stop the distribution of land that had been started. Forces had been unleashed that it was impossible to check.

The distribution of land took place on such a scale that, from the feeble beginning, it soon came to be thought that in the future the nation's agriculture would rest upon two fundamental pillars: the ejido and the small farm. This was accompanied by the conviction that the ejido would not be, as was formerly the conception, a marginal thing of little importance and almost wholly devoted to subsistence farming, but that it could be expected to make a contribution to the agricultural progress of the nation, and that it should practice commercial farming of the same type as that on the privately owned farms. The latter belief was reaffirmed from 1935 on, as the agrarian reform program affected the properties located in the richest agricultural regions of the country.

Between 1935 and 1941 the movement resembled a steam roller, and it may be said that the reform, casting aside all fear and trembling, attained its fullness. The leader of this rebirth of agrarianism was Lázaro Cárdenas, whom the simple folk of Mexico consider to be a living hero. Thereafter the chief preoccupations were directed toward preventing or neutralizing the possible ill effects of the reform by means of governmental assistance, increasingly greater and better organized, to agriculture in general and to ejido farming in particular. There were also serious attempts to direct the internal organization of the ejidos into new channels. Irrigation works, ways of communication, and agricultural credit had been begun and carried on since 1926 (ten years after the beginning of the reform); but beginning in 1936 they received a vigorous stimulus. Agricultural research was slower in developing, and well-organized work along these lines dates from 1941. The transformation of agriculture produced by all this continues to the present, and many of its aspects are spectacular. Involved in this is not merely the direct influence of the agricultural policy, but the indirect effects of industrialization, which has also received heavy official promotion. One good way to improve the agriculture of a country is by the promotion of industry.

It may be indicated that at present the agrarian mysticism has disappeared. The important agrarian activities go on by means of colonization projects. Naturally the government officials and the politicians now place much less emphasis upon satisfying the campesinos' right to the land and the destruction of the latifundia, since little remains to be done in these respects. The political line of land distribution has been exhausted. But it is necessary to keep the new landowners satisfied. Thus agrarianism has disappeared as a result of the revolution in agriculture.

The preoccupations mentioned gave rise to frequent modifications in the agrarian legislation. Actually one may distinguish two types of these [. . .]. Some of the modifications tended to amplify the rights of those soliciting land [. . .]. The second type attempted to alleviate some of the difficulties with the agrarian structure which was created by the reforms, or to place a limit upon subdivision. [. . .]

THE PRESENT SITUATION

As a result of the agrarian reform approximately 50 per cent of the arable land in Mexico was converted into ejidos, and the remainder, full-fledged private property, was divided into small and medium-sized farms. The ejido, because of its peculiarities, is the most interesting part of the new system of landholding. The ejido attained its height in 1940, and since then its relative position in the agricultural pattern has been diminishing, despite the fact that from then until now the creation of new ejidos at the expense of private holdings has continued. This is to say that from 1940 on the rate of development and expansion of privately owned farms has exceeded that of the ejidos. [. . .]

The preceding may be interpreted in the sense that the ancient struggle between private property and communal property, which has characterized the economic history of Mexico, is still going on. Present features of this struggle are not limited to the loss of relative importance by the ejido, but include indications of an extralegal process of the absorption of the ejido economy by private farming, and of a change in the nature of the ejido. Space does not permit a detailed enumeration of these indications, but the principal ones are: the utilization of the communal lands of the ejidos (the pastures and woods), not by the members of the ejidos, but by outside concessionaires; the renting of ejido lands to individual farmers; the sale of some of the tracts to individuals (keeping secret the bill of sale and noting as members of the ejido the private owners who purchase them); various forms of economic dependence of the members of the ejidos upon the individual farmers; and the monopolization of parcels within the ejidos by some of the members. To this must be added the cases of a different nature but similar meaning, through which the member of the ejido receives only a gift of his rights in the communal property, but does not participate in farming the land, which is in the hands of an official agency. Finally, there remain to be emphasized, among this type of phenomena, the parcels and ejidos that have been abandoned. [. . .]

. . .

The idea that a review of the results of the Mexican agrarian reform is needed, in order that the necessary modifications may be made, is steadily gaining strength. It is believed that this will have great importance for the economic development of agriculture and social well being, to such a degree that one may say there will be a new agrarian reform for the improvement of the earlier one. It would be well to undertake this new work slowly, by homogeneous agricultural regions, and by establishing beforehand an improvement plan for each of these regions. The principal points to include in such a plan are approximately as follows:

1. The application of agrarian programs or colonization projects to the remaining latifundia and to national lands. For this more flexible provisions are needed with respect to unaffectability, taking into account the concept of optimal economic size, the degree to which the lands affected are cultivated, and whether the owners are using them directly or indirectly.

2. The regrouping of fragmented holdings, communal or privately owned.

3. The extinction of the privately owned minifundia by promoting the necessary consolidations. This point is intimately related to the preceding one.

4. Regulations establishing that the ejidos must adopt the cooperative form of production, or continue using it, leaving in them only the minimal number of members needed relative to the resources, and organizing the cooperative work well without dividing the land into parcels. In this case the abolition of the rigidity of the man-parcel tie will consist of making it legal to sell the right to belong to these collectives, either to the collective itself (which should have the preference), or to another person of the same social type as the member, and who is approved by the collective.

5. In the ejidos which must continue to be worked as separate tracts, the sizes of the lots should be revised by increasing them to the maximum that an average family can cultivate aided by the best methods and assisted during rush

periods, but not permanently, by wage hands. [. . .]

The sale and mortgaging of the use of the parcels and the improvements between members should put a stop to the present illegal practice of renting or selling to outsiders.

6. There should be a general examination and validation of land titles, a cadastral survey, and the establishment of a rational system of taxation. Likewise there should be general examination and reconfirmation of water rights.

7. There should be a delimitation of the areas which should be reserved solely for woodlands and pastures.

8. There should be an organization of all other related activities for the better agricultural development of the region involved, such as public works, credit, technical assistance, health, and education.

16

RECENT DEVELOPMENTS IN MEXICO'S AGRARIAN REFORM PROGRAM

Víctor Manzanilla Schaffer

In December, 1958, a new phase of Mexico's agrarian reform was initiated, one that took into account the positive and negative results as well as the essential principles of the reform. The principal characteristic of this new phase is that endeavors to solve the problems of the *ejidatario* [the member of the agricultural collective or *ejido*] and of the small landowner did not continue in a piecemeal way, but are made in an integral manner as a part of the social and economic problems facing the entire nation. In other words the agrarian dynamism of the present government makes possible the application in an integrated form of each and every one of the principles of our agrarian reform for the benefit of the rural sectors of the country, an execution that is carried out in an orderly and coherent way.

Let us analyze some of the points in the agrarian program of the administration headed by Adolfo Lopez Mateos. To

Translated from Víctor Manzanilla Schaffer, *La Reforma Agraria* (México: Departamento de Asuntos Agrarios y Colonización, 1964), pp. 69-75. Printed by permission of the author.

meet the social and economic problem represented by the landless *campesinos*, acceleration was ordered in the procedures for granting or restoring land and enlarging holdings, so as to improve the situation of the campesinos in the localities in which they live. When this is impossible due to the lack of land in these localities, and except for the restoration of lands, the ejidal device designated as the creation of new population centers is used. In this way it has been possible to achieve a delivery of land amounting to 200,000 hectares per month.

The provisions of the Federal Colonization Law are applied as a complementary feature in the solution of the problems of the landless campesinos. In the new program of internal colonization the State gives preference to those ejidatarios who have unused agrarian rights [personal rights to allotments of land that have never been received or have been received only in part]. In this manner the resettlement of the excess population of the ejidos is carried out systematically and at an accelerating rate. The immediate objectives of this policy are: to destroy the *latifundia* and the monopolies of land, to cancel all the concessions of unaffectability [exemption from liability to expropriation] of pasture lands which are of dubious legality, and to utilize to the maximum the vast areas of the public domain which have long remained unproductive. Likewise, it is intended to correct past abuses in all and every one of the irrigation projects under consideration, and only genuine campesinos who hold agrarian rights shall receive parcels.

The four factors mentioned above, that is land, credit, irrigation, and technical assistance, shall, as far as possible, be included in a single legal transaction, thus avoiding the ill effects of successive procedures.

In the new agrarian dynamism and for the purpose of giving the member of the ejido a decisive initial start, pastoral ejidos are being created throughout the entire Republic, and forestry ejidos are being established in appropriate locations.

Communal possessions have been protected by the Decree of April 23, 1959, which regulates the planning, control, and supervision of the investment of the ejido's communal funds, guaranteeing the preservation and increase of the ejido's capital, that is, of the communal funds. In our opinion, in order to overcome some legal objections, it is necessary to consolidate the beneficial effects of this decree by a law that will guarantee the preservation and development of the patrimony of the ejido.

The agrarian program of the present administration, in full force, seeks to strengthen existing ejidos by respecting and increasing the agrarian rights and by stimulating social solidarity between the members of the ejidos. Their internal organization is consolidated by the promotion of democracy within the ejidos and by respect for the deliberations and resolutions of the ejido's general assembly, which is considered its supreme authority. Thus, with the firm intention of terminating caciquism, the administration from the very first has proceeded to renew the authority of all the ejidos that have complied with their mandates.

Another economic aspect that should be emphasized is the tendency to organize the ejido as an "economic unit of production." The methods employed include the following: because the areas allotted to the ejidos were inadequate, many of the parcels are very small, so it was proposed to increase the productivity of the parcels by means of technical assistance and the use of fertilizers. A decisive factor in the attainment of such an objective is the use of the spare time of the members of the ejido in other productive activities related to agriculture and stockraising, such as the improvement of the family allotment, bee culture, the raising of poultry, and so forth. This type of promotion, which the government is carrying on, is important because it is helping to transform the ejidos' agricultural activities from subsistence farming to production for the market. There are those who think it would be well for the ejido to be entirely self-sufficient; that is to say that it should have a closed economy, which was one of the characteristics of the *hacienda* during the Díaz regime. This erroneous way of thinking would lead to the segregation of the ejido system from the general economy of the nation, with all its inherent pernicious results. What is being done leads to the incorporation of the ejido system into the general system of production, distribution, and consumption of goods. In addition another point in the program is the transformation of the agricultural, pastoral, or forestry ejido into an industrial ejido.

This last point represents one of the most important tendencies of what we have called the new phase of agrarian reform. In effect the attempt is being made to incorporate the member of the ejido into the stimulation and development of the country by preparing him to perform the first activities in the processing and transformation of the products of the ejido. We ourselves believe that the first steps toward such a goal should consist primarily of fostering small household industries and, through adequate legislation, the strengthening and protection of rural crafts. Moreover, it is necessary to bring about a closer relationship between the campesinos and their products and the industry of transformation.[. . .]

From the sociological point of view, through the attainment of the objectives set forth a complete social transformation of our country will be accomplished with the elevation of the masses of our rural population into middle-class producers and consumers.

Recently a new step has been taken for the well-being of the campesinos: the establishment of social security in Mexican agriculture.

The dynamism of the present government has already produced its fruits. Latifundia have been expropriated (Cananea, Sonora; Cloete, Coahuila; and Indiviso, Baja California), simulated concessions of unaffectability have been canceled (Galindo, Querétaro; Pozo Hondo, Zacatecas; and Noria de Alday and Providencia, Guanajuato), over 200 new population centers [have been established], ejido caciques [have been] removed, and a series of other accomplishments too long to describe [have been achieved].

On the other hand we should mention that the agrarian dynamism of the government has produced no unrest in

Mexican agriculture, because it was carried on systematically within the norms pertaining to agriculture. Furthermore, the small farm devoted either to agricultural or to pastoral activities is the object of protection and support. It and the ejidos are the pillars which support our agriculture.[. . .]

We believe that the attitude and activities of the government indicate that the Mexican agrarian reform has ceased to be the banner of just one group and has become an active part of our national ideology. On the other hand its measures are no longer executed merely with a political preoccupation, but they are carried to their end in a conscientious manner so as to disseminate their valuable social and economic provisions among the nation's rural masses. In a word the essence is profoundly humanitarian.[. . .]

The fruitful accomplishments of the present government in agricultural matters assure us that the Mexican agrarian reform has entered a stage of consolidation, improvement, and perfection of its postulates for the benefit of the rural masses of the nation and the economic development of the country.

The first part of the activities of the agrarian reform, the redistribution of the ownership of rural property, has proved to be a decisive factor in the social and economic equilibrium of Mexico. At present the government presses forward in the accomplishment of what we have designated the new phase, that is, the second part in the execution of the basic principles of agrarian reform. This part consists primarily of consolidating and organizing the internal affairs of the ejidos with the objective of making them into true economic units of production.

17

THE OBJECTIVES OF AGRARIAN
REFORM IN VENEZUELA

❧

ARTICLE 1. The objective of the present Law is the transformation of the nation's agrarian structure and the incorporation of its rural population into the economic, social, and political development of the country through the replacement of the *latifundia* system by a just system of property, tenure, and use of the land, based upon an equitable distribution of the same, an adequate organization of credit, and integrated assistance to the rural producers, so that the land shall be for the one who works it the basis of his economic stability, the foundation of his progressive social well-being, and the guarantee of his liberty and dignity.

ARTICLE 2. In order to comply with the purposes indicated, this Law:

(a) Guarantees and regulates the right to private ownership of the land, in conformity with the principle of the social function which the same should fulfill and in accord-

Translated from *Ley de Reforma Agraria* (Caracas: Publicaciones Nacionales, March, 1960), pp. 3-5.

ance with the other regulations established in the Constitution and the laws;

(b) Guarantees the right of every individual or group of people who are suited for work in agriculture or stockraising and who lack land or have insufficient amounts of it to be given the ownership of lands that are suited for economic utilization, preferably in the areas in which they work or live, or, when circumstances make it advisable, in carefully selected zones, and subject to the limits and norms established by this Law;

(c) Guarantees the right of the agriculturists to own the land which they are cultivating under the terms and conditions foreseen by this Law;

(d) Takes cognizance of the Indian population which retains a communal state or one of the extended family, and without prejudice to the rights they have as Venezuelans, in accordance with the preceding provisions, guarantees their right to make use of the lands, forests, and waters which they occupy or which belong to the places in which they live habitually without prejudice to their incorporation into national life in accordance with this and other laws;

(e) [Guarantees] to favor and protect in a special way the development of the small and the medium-sized rural properties and the agricultural cooperatives so that they shall come to be stable and efficient.

For this purpose, the right to the small family-sized farm is established in accordance with the norms relative to gratuitous grants contained in this Law.

ARTICLE 3. The obligations arising from the principle of the social function of landownership shall apply both to the individual and to the State.

ARTICLE 4. For purposes of the dispositions in part (b) of Article 2, the State shall incorporate into the economic development of the country, in a progressive manner, those zones or regions that are deficiently used or inaccessible, due to the lack of ways of communication, irrigation works, safeguards to health, and so forth.

For these purposes [the State] shall promote plans for the integral development of economic or hydrographic regions, but in any case the plans for the development and use of water resources and for agricultural and pastoral development should be conceived in terms of integral development and should be in accord with the plans for agrarian reform.

ARTICLE 5. The State shall establish and increase the public services that are necessary and adequate for the transformation of the rural areas and for assistance to agricultural and livestock producers who comply with the obligations arising from the social function of property and comply with the obligations which this Law imposes upon them.

ARTICLE 6. In the Law of the General Budget of Public Receipts and Expenditures, assignments shall be made for the financing of the agrarian reform and subsequent agricultural planning.

ARTICLE 7. The State is obligated to create the bases and conditions required for the dignification of the work of the agricultural wage hand, through an adequate regulation of the same and of its juridical aspects in accordance with the changes that shall result from the agrarian reform.

ARTICLE 8. In the conditions that have been established, foreigners shall enjoy equal rights with the Venezuelans and shall be submitted to the same obligations with respect to all of the matters which constitute the object of this Law.

ARTICLE 9. Persons having the right to request a grant of land are authorized to present information relative to lands which are not complying with their social function.

This denouncement shall be made before the appropriate Delegation and this, within a period of thirty (30) days, shall make the necessary investigations and shall inform the one making the denouncement.

If the denouncement is justified, the lands shall be subject to acquisition or expropriation in accordance with the present Law.

18

THE SOCIAL FUNCTION
OF PROPERTY
Orlando Fals Borda

[During the Seminar on "Land Problems in Latin America,"
held in Montevideo in November and December, 1959, under the auspices of the Food and Agriculture Organization
and the Government of Uruguay, Dr. Orlando Fals Borda,
the delegate from Colombia, presented the following exposition relating to the social function of property.

The exposition gave rise to a heated debate among the
participants, and a special session was organized to discuss
it. At the conclusion of the debate, the delegates from Mexico and Chile proposed that the text be presented as a declaration of principles which could be adopted by all the
American nations as an ideological basis for genuine agrarian reform.]

Great controversies have arisen with respect to the concept of the social function of property. Does the proprietor

Translated from *La Función Social de la Propiedad*, Mimeographed
(Montevideo: December 1959). Printed by permission of the
author.

or the user of land have an obligation to use it in a way that will contribute to the general welfare of society? Or should property be considered as a simple gift that is justified by natural class distinctions?

Strange as it may seem, the concept of the social function of property, which today is presented as one of the possible justifications for agrarian reform, has its roots in the cosmogonic and philosophical concept which maintains that man must answer to the Creator for the use of the resources and elements entrusted to him. It is an old concept and it is intimately related to the genesis of society itself.

At the dawn of civilization the mere possession of the land constituted the basis of political power; the sense of equity in the distribution of the same began to arise only in the days of Lycurgus, and it soon was to be lost again. The fact of having added to the concept of "possession" that of good social use of the possession was of itself a genuine revolution which was given expression in part in the writings of philosophers and thinkers such as Seneca and St. Ambrose. Indeed, one may ask why should land be placed in a different category from other natural elements such as water, air, and light? Does it not belong (or should it not belong) to all of humanity? These are the same arguments that various persons have recently advanced with respect to the matters involved.

As we understand it, the Spaniards were the first to employ and to introduce in America the concept of the social function of property, in terms such as might be envied by contemporary advocates of agrarian reform. In effect, as soon as they settled the controversy as to whether or not the lands of the New World belonged to the Indians, the personal occupation and use of the land became a requirement for the confirmation of land grants. And this requirement could not be met in just any way. The Spanish colonist had to remain in the settlement a specified number of years, construct a dwelling, and make plantings of subsistence crops. Doubtless many of the *ecomenderos* and potentates became masters who exploited the local workers, creating *latifundia* which remain today as a dead weight upon the national economies. But it cannot be denied that Spain was also developing a class of artisans and farmers on our continent, one that was charged with producing and maintaining physically the remainder of the society by means of the small and the medium-sized property, the origin of our *minifundia*. The Spanish government periodically proceeded to make adjustments of the lands in the Indian reservations to determine, among other things, whether or not the land was being used; in the negative case, it reverted to the State or was sold to persons who promised to make use of it.

The requirements of the Spanish government were founded precisely in the cosmic philosophy, of which I have spoken, as this took juridical form in the papal bull, "Inter Coetera," of 1494, and the resulting concept of "eminent domain" of the State, a concept which all of our governments inherited from Spain. This is the concept which justifies the intervention of the State in the expropriation of land when it is necessary for certain purposes, or when the land is not complying with its social function; this is to say, when the owners do not know how to, are unable to, or do not care to make use of the land, as God's stewards, in order to promote the general welfare and progress of the society to which they belong.

If we define the social function of property in this way, one can well understand the eagerness of many governments, including that of Colombia, to make use of this formula to justify their intervention in the use of badly utilized, privately owned lands. Thus it is employed in Colombia's National Constitution, which states that "all property involves a social function," and further provides that prior to the expropriation of land, this should be declared of "public utility." The State's right of eminent domain, therefore, receives its most dynamic use for purposes of collective benefits. For example, it is evident that the interests of the collectivity are observed to be affected adversely by the latifundistas, who leave in idleness lands which they own that adjoin roads and railroads, or are located on the outskirts of cities, strangling the latter and adding to the costs of agricultural products. Or the owners may be devoting their lands to extensive, poorly cared for, and poorly managed uses, alongside of lands that are being cultivated intensively. This is prejudicial; therefore, a change in the situation is required. In addition, the owners may have extensive holdings that are far away and covered with virgin forests which they possess merely in expectation that a road will be built and that they will obtain the unearned increment on its increase in value. Or, finally, a large landowner may be exploiting not merely the land, but also his sharecroppers and other workers by means of excessive, abusive, semi-feudal contracts, producing situations of poverty and ignorance that are contrary to the labor legislation of the various countries and which are intolerable for the societies involved. Above all, these kinds of proprietors (the latifundistas, the anti-technical, the absentee, and the feudal) should have to feel the weight of the law, because their lands do not reach the point of complying with the social function expected of them, and come to form a real or potential obstacle for all of society.

It is realized that the concept may involve some confusion from the technical point of view, although it is clear from the historical and religious standpoints. In Colombia various efforts have been made to give it a technical content, or at least a more precise and pragmatic one. The most dramatic and revolutionary of all these is that expressed in the definitions in Articles 1 and 2 of Law 200 of 1936, where the social function was interpreted as if it meant the economic utilization of the land, declaring that all lands which did not exhibit evidences of such utilization was presumed to be *baldíos* [in the public domain]. Unfortunately, the definition of economic utilization in Law 200 was not sufficiently specific, an omission which left it practically without force.

Lately there have been attempts to interpret the concept of economic utilization on the basis of the typical uses of various kinds of soils. The progress of the soil sciences and their application in Colombia have permitted a new and practical interpretation of the social function of property in a manner that has gained concrete expression in various decrees and laws (Decree 290 of 1957, and Law 20 of 1959) on the minimal requirements of rational use of the land. Especially emphasized is the system of setting forth general regulations pertaining to how the land should be used, what crops should be planted, what should be preserved, etc., including the social and economic aspects, in the specific regions. During the last three months the government has advanced along these lines. When a person uses his property badly, that is to say when it is not complying with its social function, the government may require him to comply with it by means of the general regulations. Furthermore, if the owner does not conform with the provisions of these regulations, or if it has not been possible to resolve the social problem involved, the State still retains its right to expropriate.

Following along these lines in Colombia various *haciendas* have been purchased or expropriated for purposes of subdivision and a large colonization program has been commenced. A weighty reason has propelled the governments during the last twenty years to proceed in this manner to give a practical sense to the concept of the social function of property. This reason is that the number of the dispossessed has been rising and the pressures for land have increased considerably. A late complication has been the awakening of the rural masses with new desires and demands. The end of the feudal regime which the Spaniards bequeathed to us has required rapid and effective action by the State. Because the *campesinos* previously were and even now are exploited and depreciated, upon eating of the fruit of the tree of knowledge they have discovered that they are naked, in relation to the class of large landowners who direct affairs, and they do not enjoy the obvious lack of equality.

Thus, we conclude that the problem of the social function of property, although originally religious and dressed in juridical robes, is in reality a technical matter with human implications. It would be unwise for a lawyer to apply simple, traditional formulas to a problem of such complexity. The modern world, to overcome a possible Malthusian menace, needs the efficient and intelligent use of all availa-

ble resources. If privately owned lands, the greatest of all resources, remain unused or poorly used, those responsible for
it are committing a crime against society. Unfortunately,
many landowners do not think so and they prefer to have
land solely that it may serve as an asylum for their capital
or in order to maintain their social prestige. Experience
teaches that if the State does not take a hand in this matter
by means of its right of eminent domain in order to produce
a solution in a constructive way, the campesinos involved
will take matters into their own hands. Thus, through force
will be effected the desire of St. Ambrose that the land
should in reality be a collective patrimony for the well-being
and progress of all. Only, as we all know, in the latter case,
the victory of the revolting masses may be no more than a
Pyrrhic victory.

19

SOME BASIC ASPECTS OF AGRARIAN REFORM IN LATIN AMERICA

The Inter-American Committee for Agricultural Development

Bearing in mind that the term agrarian reform has certain highly controversial meanings, it was decided, with a view to keeping the discussion properly focused, to construe it as a series of measures designed to alter present agrarian structures, including change in the legal relation between man and the land, with a view to obtaining a more effective use of resources and a higher and more equitably distributed average income.

The following conclusions, grouped according to the guide lines governing the discussion, can be drawn from the experts' statements:

A. PRESENT AGRARIAN STRUCTURES AND THEIR RELATION TO ECONOMIC DEVELOPMENT

It was unanimously agreed that present systems of land tenure which in most countries are marked by unequal, in-

From Inter-American Committee for Agricultural Development, *Meeting of High Level Experts in Agricultural Problems* (Washington, D. C.: Pan American Union, 1962), pp. 16-23. Reprinted by permission of the Committee.

equitable distribution of ownership, give rise to a series of economic and social problems that, directly or indirectly, are impeding speedier development of agriculture and the economy in general. The execution of an agrarian reform that would lead to alteration of the legal relationship between man and the land so as to secure a more equitable distribution of wealth and higher levels of production, productivity and living is therefore a key factor in expediting the economic and social development of most Latin American countries.

It was made clear that the execution of agrarian reform entails a sweeping overhaul of the entire economic, social, and political structure that now prevails in the agricultural sector and that poses a series of problems that must be solved if the desired objectives are to be achieved. Highly urgent complementary measures, such as the bringing of larger areas under cultivation, education, agricultural credit, technical assistance, capital investment in agricultural activities and infrastructural works, research, expansion of agricultural cooperatives, and improved methods of processing and marketing are imperative. It must also be kept in mind that agrarian reform should not be regarded solely as a mechanism for increasing agricultural productivity and heightening its efficiency; rather, it must be considered as having a much broader aim than the achievement of this objective, and that increasing and redistributing income, educating the rural population, and so forth, serve as the basis of economic development.

It was also pointed out that in most Latin American countries a high proportion of the economically active population was in the agricultural sector, which showed a high rate of unemployment and under-employment. There was slight prospect of agriculture providing full employment for these people, and even though there was a large area of uncultivated land in many countries, the investments necessary to place these new lands under cultivation and the slowness of this process offered no solution to the problem of relocating a substantial portion of the surplus population. It was equally out of the question to consider the possibility of subdividing landholdings already under cultivation in such [a] way as to enable all the rural workers to become landowners; such a procedure would create a serious new hazard of excessive subdivision of the land, which would preclude all possibility of efficient exploitation. It was felt to be absolutely essential, therefore, that agrarian reform programs be closely integrated with agricultural development and general development programs, which would allow suitable complementarity between the agricultural sector and the rest of the economy, with the objective, among others, of diverting the economically active rural population into other sectors.

It was taken for granted that most Latin American countries intend to carry out agrarian reforms and that these should be executed in an evolutionary manner and be so planned as to avoid abrupt changes that would lead to the collapse of systems of production and an abrupt decline in crop volume. However, it must be kept in mind that there is a great social unrest among the rural population, and that this can be allayed only through speedy and drastic evolution. It was accordingly agreed that many measures being considered as effective means for compelling land redistribution, without need for resorting to more radical and direct action, are merely rather ineffectual palliatives and should be regarded as steps complementary to agrarian reform, rather than [as] means of achieving it. Special emphasis was placed on the matter of tax policies designed to impose more effective land taxes and compel the owners either to work their land or relinquish it to others who can do so better. The enforcement of such measures should be considered rather as a prerequisite for agrarian reform, since it would tend to eliminate speculative land prices and serve as a means to promote agricultural development.

The redistribution of land rights, accompanied by all measures that would facilitate a rise in the levels of productivity, production, and living for the rural worker, seems to be the sole means of achieving an adequate redistribution of agricultural wealth and income, and in turn eliminating the political power of the landowners. It was also decided that a redistribution of land rights did not necessarily imply a breaking up of physical property, and that there were various ways of achieving the desired objectives of agrarian reform without the necessity of subdividing the existing landholdings now in operation.

It was made clear that, among the objectives of agrarian reform, priority should be given to enhancing the human dignity of the rural worker and thus enabling him to make a greater contribution to the improvement of society.

B. POSSIBILITY OF CARRYING OUT OVERALL AGRARIAN REFORM IN STAGES

There was general agreement that any agrarian reform should be of an overall nature if it is to produce the desired social, economic and political effects. Accordingly, the laws instituting agrarian reform should cover the entire country and should be applied as expeditiously as possible. It was noted, however, that most of the countries are scarcely in a position to carry out this purpose now, because of the lack of adequate studies of their countries' various agricultural regions, a dearth of funds and, above all, a shortage of trained personnel to perform all the preliminary operations necessary to ensure the success of the reform. A law of this nature cannot consider an entire country as a homogeneous unit, but should envisage the application to each region or district of such measures as, taking due account of the prevalent land tenure situation, would be best suited to the essential features of its agriculture, the population pressure on the land, the ethnic and social composition of the population, the situation in the non-agricultural sectors of the economy, and so forth. Thus, it is possible that in practice agrarian reform will have to be carried out by regions in successive geographical areas, and that the steps to be taken will also be carried out in stages.

It was emphasized particularly that, in order to avoid a sudden decline in production in the areas affected, prompt emergency measures should be taken to extend to those benefiting from the reform, all necessary services to enable them to adjust to their new status as owners. These services should include agricultural extension, technological factors and credit facilities, processing and marketing services, and the like. In the areas not affected by direct reform, special arrangements must be made to enable the large land-holders to maintain production and substantially improve working relations of the rural workers or, in the contrary case, relinquish their land to other persons capable of operating them satisfactorily from the two points of view: economic and social.

Another important factor limiting the speed with which the redistribution of land rights can be effected is the possibility of finding, selecting, and training the new entrepreneurs. A suggestion was offered whereby, in addition to the usual procedures of selection and training, the land-holdings would be turned over to the beneficiaries for probationary periods of four to five years, after which they would keep for cultivation only as much land as they had been able to cultivate successfully.

C. COMPATIBILITY OF THE SOCIAL-POLITICAL IMPROVEMENT OBJECTIVES OF AGRARIAN REFORM WITH THE DEMANDS OF OPTIMUM MOBILIZATION OF RESOURCES AIMED TO ACHIEVE MAXIMUM PRODUCTION

It was unanimously agreed that the first objective of agrarian reform would be essentially of a social nature, and once this was achieved, attainment of the economic objectives would be possible. It must be kept constantly in mind that the cost of failure to take steps to modify the agrarian structures is, in the long run, much greater than any price that might be paid for carrying out the necessary reform. Social unrest, infant mortality, rural want, unemployment, loss of natural resources, and stagnation of production are only a few of the problems that will be perpetuated if resolute action is not taken with regard to agrarian reform.

It was made clear, however, that the majority of the Latin American countries are in an exceptional position to combine these social and economic criteria, since in many regions the population pressure on the land is not very strong, and even where it is, there are possibilities for reducing it by bringing new land under cultivation. However, it is the unused or improperly used land of the very large estates and government-owned properties that offer an excellent means of attaining these objectives.

Redistribution of land rights or the division of large properties must inevitably result in a change in the systems of operation and types of production, which can bring about a decline in production, particularly if these changes are made quickly and are unaccompanied by the measures necessary to supplement them. However, this situation can be quickly changed, if proper guidance is provided to direct the operations toward more intensive types of operations. It was noted that, thanks to modern technology, it is now possible to achieve effective combinations of resources and high efficiency even on small landholdings. Care will have to be exercised to ensure that the increased production will keep ahead of the increased consumption that the new situation will engender among the beneficiaries of agrarian reform, and thus prevent a drop in the volume of production flowing into the customary channels.

D. POSSIBILITIES OF FINANCING AGRARIAN REFORM. CRITERIA TO GOVERN LAND EXPROPRIATION

There were divergent opinions on this subject, particularly with regard to the form of expropriation. Although some experts held that land that is badly used, that is, that does not serve its social purpose, should automatically be returned to the state, without compensation, the majority felt that it was possible to respect land ownership rights and, where expropriation is made, this could be done in accordance with previously established and effectively applied legal principles. The opinion was also expressed that compensation for expropriated land should not be at the prevailing market prices. Various alternatives were suggested for inducing a drop in land prices and thus reduce the amount of compensation. Application of an appropriate tax policy prior to the reform would cause a sharp drop in prices. It was further suggested that expropriation prices be based on the capitalized value of the income from the land during the five-year period preceding the reform.

There was complete concurrence, with regard to financing land purchases, that it was impossible to pay cash for the land, as stipulated by the constitutions of several Latin American countries. In countries where it is possible to make deferred payment for expropriated land, to encourage investment it might be established, for instance, that bonds issued for this purpose could be redeemed at once and at par, for two specific purposes: (1) reinvestment in the particular farm in question or in agriculture in general, with a view to intensifying exploitation and improving productivity; and (2) investment in given industries determined by the government. Such an investment system should be accompanied by a suitable income-tax system, to allow the government to obtain part of the profits the new agrarian structure yields.

As to financing for the other sectors of the reform, especial emphasis was laid on the need of placing at its disposal all economic means for making the necessary capital investments in infrastructural works and providing various services to the beneficiaries. The suggestion was also made that it would be advisable to seek foreign loans to supplement national efforts to finance investment required.

E. THE POSSIBLE EFFECTS ON THE BENEFICIARY OF AGRARIAN REFORM OF THE RADICAL CHANGE IN HIS SOCIAL AND ECONOMIC STATUS IN HIS PASSAGE FROM THE POSITION OF A LANDLESS RURAL WORKER TO THAT OF A LANDOWNER OR ENTREPRENEUR. MEANS OF SOLVING THE PROBLEMS THAT MAY ARISE

The problems relating to this point vary drastically, depending on the cultural level, income level, land tenure system, labor systems, degree of individual freedom, and the like, peculiar to the beneficiary. If we consider most of the Latin American countries, it will be noted that the living and educational levels of the rural worker are generally so low that they are most unlikely to possess the technical knowledge or administrative ability necessary to assume the responsibilities that will devolve upon them as beneficiaries of agrarian reform. The tenant farmers, sharecroppers, owner-operators of minifundia, and even those workers receiving a small tract of land as wage payments will be in a better position, since they will have at least some managerial experience. The landless workers, especially those working in specialized types of operations (plantations) are particularly at a disadvantage if the reform is based exclusively in the creation of family-farms.

It will be necessary in all cases to make a painstaking selection of the future beneficiaries, and to provide them with extensive educational, technical, and economic assistance in order to prevent a sharp drop in production and, most particularly, to give them incentives to rise in the social and economic scale. This educational effort should be started, where possible, before the reform.

It was suggested, as a highly effective measure to help achieve these objectives, that the land not be handed over for outright ownership, but rather [that it be] given on a long-term, even inheritable, lease, which would remain in force only so long as the land was well exploited, within clearly defined limits. Special emphasis was given to the fact that what is of interest to the rural worker is not so much land ownership as security of tenure.

The importance, in connection with solving some of the problems arising from agrarian reform, of the cooperative movement and of the establishment of producers' associations as a supplement to the agricultural extension work to be provided was pointed out.

Mention was also made of the great advantages to be derived from collective and cooperative systems of operations as solutions to the problem of rapidly training owner-operators.

In conclusion, statements were made on the urgent need for taking steps in any agrarian reform program to prevent persons outside the field of agriculture from taking advantage of the situation to obtain land that would then lie idle.

F. FORMS OF LAND TENURE OTHER THAN PRIVATE OWNERSHIP THAT COULD BE TRIED OUT IN LATIN AMERICA, AND THE ADVANTAGES THEREOF. POSSIBILITIES OF REGROUPING MINIFUNDIA

Two quite different views were expressed in the experts' remarks on this point. While on the one hand there was a very positive emphasis on the need to maintain private ownership, and within that, the family-size farm, on the other there was an equally strong affirmation of the desirability of adjusting the systems of land tenure to the traditions and experiences of the peoples of the hemisphere and adopting flexible systems conducive to a solution of the many problems of underdevelopment besetting the region.

Adduced in support of the first viewpoint were the advantages that the family-size farm has for the individual, mainly because it gives him an incentive to forge ahead and enjoy to the fullest the fruits of his own and his family's work. Among other arguments in support of this system, the most telling were the disadvantages that would be encountered by the cooperative and collective systems when operating in the Latin American agricultural environment. Attention was called particularly to the possibility that the establishment of collective or cooperative type of farms might result, if adequate control were not maintained over the actions of the officials concerned therewith, in simply exchanging the feudalism of large landowners for state feudalism. Also underscored was the difficulty of instilling mutual trust among the members of a cooperative, and of obtaining cooperative leaders capable of administering productive units of this nature. There was agreement, however, that absolute and total ownership of the land, without restrictions that would compel its conservation and prevent its progressive subdivision, could have very serious consequences for the countries of the region.

The proponents of the second viewpoint insisted that most of the Latin American peoples have ancestral traditions favorable to the establishment of communal, cooperative, or collective systems of work and operation. Moreover, the rural worker's low level of education and living would hinder his rapid conversion into an efficient, ambitious owner-operator. Only through these systems would it be possible to increase his efficiency and productivity, to the benefit of himself and the collectivity. These systems would also have a decided advantage in those areas where there is population pressure on the land, since they would be the only way of achieving better use of resources, including manpower. It should also be kept in mind that in the present circumstances, the large land-owner is virtually the government and the organizer of economic and social activity in many regions, and when he disappears a vacuum will result that, unless filled by responsible organizations and leaders, could produce chaos. The aforementioned organizations provide a desirable solution to this problem.

The drawbacks of breaking up large units were emphasized in which a close complementary relationship exists between land of different climates and different kinds of cultivation, since if this were done, these advantages would be lost, with consequent destruction of the established systems. Here again the cooperative system would help to maintain an operation of this type, with resultant advantages accruing to the new users, particularly to the landless farm workers.

There was general agreement on the desirability of establishing mixed systems in keeping with the socio-economic and demographic characteristics of each region, endeavoring in all cases to avoid the cession of absolute ownership rights to the land.

G. APPLICATION OF COMMUNITY DEVELOPMENT TECHNIQUES IN LATIN AMERICA

This is unquestionably one of the best measures to complement agrarian reform, because of the effect it may have in the preparatory training of the beneficiaries in their new responsibilities, and in the training and organization of rural leaders to replace the former landowners in guiding the local community. The importance of this measure for the success of the agrarian reform program must be kept well in mind, since it has been observed that if the rural inhabitants manage to organize themselves adequately under the leadership of qualified persons, they will have great advantages for raising their standards of living and improving their technical efficiency. These organizations should receive unstinted government support with regard to their needs for credit, technical assistance, educational and health facilities, and the like.

One group felt, however, that a precise definition of the regulations and standards to govern communal programs in Latin America is needed. At the present time, there is no clear picture of the type of communal programs that can really be carried out with the active participation of the communities themselves, or of the possible effects of such programs on agriculture.

BIBLIOGRAPHY

The titles in this bibliography have been carefully selected. Even though they total slightly more than 150, they represent merely a small fraction of the items thoroughly pertinent to the subject that might have been included. Such a list seems especially short if it is compared with those in the two most comprehensive bibliographies in the field, one edited by Accioly Borges and the other compiled and edited by Carroll, which contain 1,164 and 1,072 items, respectively. Moreover, the titles included here are by no means limited to those given in these two excellent sources.

In determining specifically which publications to include, out of the welter of possibilities, there were many complexities to be faced and many decisions, some of them rather arbitrary, to be taken. Perhaps a brief mention of some of the basic criteria used and of exceptions made will enable the reader to evaluate more adequately the results of the endeavor. First, it was considered essential to give preference to items that may be said to have professional standing—represented by the books, monographs, and articles in recognized journals in such fields as economics, history, geography, and sociology—over those that appeared in newspapers or in popular magazines, or the many that have been circulated merely in mimeographed form.

Next, it was thought preferable to concentrate largely upon publications of a substantative nature, to which the reader might go for additional analysis and description of problems and programs, rather than to use much of the space for bibliographies, guides, and other aids to research. The two most recent and comprehensive bibliographies were included, however, because they are lists that greatly surpass and outmode all earlier compilations.

Because the bulk of the pertinent material is of recent origin, a preference was given to studies published since 1950. Nevertheless, an intensive search was made for earlier background materials, and a considerable number of the more significant early items was included. Likewise, despite the fact that much of what has been published on the subject of agrarian reform in Latin America deals with matters in Brazil, Mexico, and Colombia (for which Carroll includes 184, 106, and 75 titles, respectively, in contrast with only 4 for the Dominican Republic and 7 for Panama), an attempt was made to represent all of the widely divergent sections of Latin America.

It was assumed that most of those who read this volume will find additional reading on the subject of agrarian reform more accessible and more useable if the materials are in English. Therefore, in this bibliography preference was given to books, monographs, and articles written in that language. Even so, however, the predominance of those who write in Spanish or Portuguese, among those who have made fundamental contributions to the exposition of matters related to agrarian reform in Latin America, is so great that approximately two-thirds of all the items in our list are available only in one or the other of these languages.

Finally, particular attention was given to the inclusion in this compilation of titles to works by Latin American economists, historians, geographers, and sociologists who have established enviable reputations for competency in their respective fields, and to works by their fellows in the United States and Europe whose names have come to figure prominently in the study of Latin American peoples and societies.

In conclusion it should be indicated that many of the books in our list themselves contain substantial and selected bibliographies relating to land tenure and the size of agricultural holdings, to the highly institutionalized and frequently antiquated systems used for extracting products from the soil in parts of Latin America, to locality groupings and community organization and development, and to other mat-

ters closely related to agrarian reform in the area under con-
sideration. In this respect the books by such authors as Fals
Borda, Fernández y Fernández, Ford, Horne, Leonard, Mc-
Bride, Mendieta y Núñez, Nelson, Senior, Smith, C. C.
Taylor, and Whetten are especially valuable.

Accioly Borges, Pompeu, ed., *Bibliografía sôbre Reforma
Agrária*. Rio de Janeiro: Instituto de Ciências Sociais,
Universidade de Brasil, 1962.

Acción Sindical Chilena, *Tierra y Libertad por la Reforma
Agraria*. Santiago: Acción Sindical Chilena, 1961.

Adams, Richard N., "Freedom and Reform in Rural Latin
America," in Frederic B. Pike, ed., *Freedom and Reform
in Latin America*. Notre Dame, Ind.: University of Notre
Dame Press, 1959, pp. 203-230.

Aguilez Berlioz, Rodolfo, *Régimes Agrarios*. Guatemala:
Talleres de la Tipografía Nacional de Guatemala, 1953.

Alexander, Robert J., "Agrarian Reform in Latin America."
Foreign Affairs, Vol. 41, No. 1 (October, 1962), pp.
191-207.

———— *The Bolivian National Revolution*. New Brunswick,
N.J.: Rutgers University Press, 1958.

Antezana, E. Luis, *Resultados de la Reforma Agraria en
Bolivia*. Cochabamba: F. O. Cuenca Sucs., 1955.

Arze-Loureiro, Eduardo, *Actitudes Sociales Relacionadas
con la Reforma Agraria en Bolivia* (Mimeographed). Caracas: Escuela de Ciencias Económicas, Universidad Central de Venezuela, 1958.

Balderrama G., Adalid, *La Reforma Agraria y la Experien-
cia Boliviana*. La Paz: Editorial del Estado, 1959.

Barbero, Guiseppe, "Realizaciones y Problemas de la Reforma Agraria en Bolivia." *El Trimestre Económico*
(México), Vol. XXVIII, No. 4 (Octubre-Diciembre,
1961), pp. 612-650.

Barros, Henrique de, A *Estrutura Agrária como Obstáculo
à Ação Agronômica; a Reforma Agrária como Problema
Econômico*. São Paulo: Escola de Sociología e Política,
1954.

Bauta, Juan F., "Posibilidades Constitucionales y Legales de la Redistribución de Tierras en América Latina." *Revista Interamericana de Ciencias Sociales,* Vol. 2, No. 1 (1963), pp. 5-28.

Bernhard, Guillermo, *La Reforma Agraria en los Países Latinoamericanos.* Montevideo: Imprenta García, 1962.

Beyer, Robert Carlyle, "Land Distribution and Tenure in Colombia." *Journal of Inter-American Studies* (Gainesville, Fla.), Vol. III, No. 2 (April, 1961), pp. 281-290.

Bonilla, Frank, "Rural Reform in Brazil." *Dissent,* Vol. IX, No. 4 (1962), pp. 373-382.

Brazil, Comissão Nacional de Política Agrária, *Reforma Agrária no Brasil, Estudos e Projectos.* Rio de Janeiro: Editora e Grafica Guarany Ltda., 1956.

Cardoso, Fernando Henrique, "Tensões Sociais no Campo e Reforma Agrária." *Revista Brasileira de Estudos Políticos,* No. 12 (October, 1961), pp. 7-26.

Carranza, Carlos P., *Reforma Agraria en Argentina.* Buenos Aires: Edit. Asociación Argentina por la Libertad de la Cultura, 1961.

Carroll, Thomas F., "The Land Reform Issue in Latin America," in Albert O. Hirschman, ed., *Latin American Issues.* New York: The Twentieth Century Fund, 1961.

——— *Land Tenure and Land Reform in Latin America: A Selected Bibliography (Régimen de Tierras y Reforma Agraria en América Latina; una Bibliografía Anotada de Carácter Selectivo).* Washington, D. C.: Inter-American Development Bank, 1962.

——— ed., *La Creación de Nuevas Unidades Agrícolas* (Informe del II Seminario Latino-Americano sobre Problemas de la Tierra, Montevideo). Santiago: Regional Office for Latin America of the Food and Agriculture Organization, 1961.

Centro de Investigaciones Sociales, *Primer Seminario de la Reforma Agraria.* Cuadernos 1, 2, 3, and 4. Bogotá: Centro de Investigaciones Sociales, 1963 and 1964.

Cleofas, João, *Reforma Agrária no Brasil.* Recife: Instituto Joaquím Nabuco de Pesquisas Sociais, 1960.

Colombia, Ministerio de Agricultura, *Reforma Social Agraria.* Bogotá: Imprenta Nacional, 1961.

Conforti, Emilio A., *Colonización, Reforma Agraria, Migraciones Internas.* Quito: Junta Nacional de Planificación y Coordinación Económica, 1960.

Conselho Superior das Classes Produtoras, *Reforma Agrária Brasileira.* Rio de Janeiro: Conselho Superior das Classes Produtoras, 1960.

Cook, Hugh L., "The New Agrarian Reform Law and Economic Development in Venezuela." *Land Economics* (Madison, Wisconsin) Vol. XXXVII, No. 1 (February, 1961), pp. 5-17.

Cordero Michel, José Ramón E., "Datos sobre la Reforma Agraria en la República Dominicana." *Caribbean Studies* (Puerto Rico), Vol. II, No. 1 (April, 1962), pp. 23-33.

Corvalan, Luis, *Cosas Nuevas en el Campo.* Santiago (Chile): Imprenta Lautaro, 1960 (?).

Coutinho Cavalcanti, *Um Projeto de Reforma Agrária.* Rio de Janeiro: Instituto Nacional do Livro, 1959, 2 vols.

Crossley, J. C., "Agrarian Reform in Latin America." *The Yearbook of World Affairs,* London: Stevens and Sons Limited, 1963, pp. 123-149.

Cuba, Republic of, *Land Reform Law.* Havana: Office of the Prime Minister of Cuba, 1959.

Delgado, Oscar, "La Reforma Agraria: América Latina Frente a su Destino." *Cuadernos* (Paris), No. 53 (1961), pp. 55-67.

———— "Revolution, Reform, Conservatism: Three Types of Agrarian Structure." *Dissent,* Vol. IX, No. 4 (1962), pp. 350-363.

De Young, Maurice, *Man and Land in the Haitian Economy.* Gainesville: University of Florida Press, 1958.

Diégues, Manuel, Jr., "Antecedentes da Reforma Agrária no Brasil." *Cuadernos Brasileiros* (Rio de Janeiro), Ano V, No. 4 (Julho-Agosto, 1963), pp. 51-54.

———— *População e Propriedade da Terra no Brasil.* Washington, D. C.: Pan American Union, 1959.

Duarte, Néstor, *Reforma Agrária.* Rio de Janeiro: Serviço de Documentação do MES, 1953.

Dúran, Marco Antonio, *Del Agrarismo a la Revolución Agrícolo.* México: Talleres Gráficos de la Nación, 1947.

———— "La Reforma Agraria en Cuba." *El Trimestre Económico* (México), Vol. XXVII, No. 107 (1960), pp. 410-469.

———— *Los Sofismas de la Reforma Agraria.* México: Liga de Agrónomos Socialistas, 1939.

Erasmus, Charles, *Man Takes Control.* Minneapolis: University of Minnesota Press, 1961.

Escobar, Romulo, *El Problema Agrario.* El Paso: Imprenta Juarez, 1915.

Fals Borda, Orlando, *El Hombre y la Tierra en Boyacá: Bases Socio-Históricas para una Reforma Agraria.* Bogotá: Ediciones Documentos Colombianos, 1957. (Manuscript of original English text submitted as a Ph.D. Dissertation under the title *A Sociological Study of the Relationships Between Man and the Land in the Department of Boyacá, Colombia* to the Graduate Council of the University of Florida, 1955.)

————"La Reforma Agraria," in *Memoria: VI Congreso Latinoamericano de Sociología,* Tomo II. Caracas: Imprenta Nacional, 1961, pp. 229-237.

———— "La Reforma Agraria." *Revista de la Academia Colombiana de Ciencias Exactas, Físicas y Naturales,* Vol. XI, No. 42 (1960), pp. 93-97.

Fernández y Fernández, Ramón, "La Reforma Agraria Mexicana: Logros y Problemas Derivados." *Boletín de Estudios Especiales* (México: Banco Nacional de Crédito Ejidal), Vol. VIII, No. 93 (July, 1957), pp. 211-220.

———— *Reforma Agraria en Venezuela.* Caracas: Las Novedades, 1948.

———— "Reforma Agraria en el Ecuador." *El Trimestre Económico* (México), Vol. XXVII (4), No. 112 (Octubre-Diciembre, 1961), pp. 569-594.

———— *Economía Agrícola y Reforma Agraria.* México: Centro de Estudios Monetarios Latinoamericanos, Gráfica Panamericana, 1962.

———— "Land Tenure in Mexico." *Journal of Farm Economics,* Vol. XXV, No. 1 (February, 1943), pp. 219-234.

Ferragut, Castro, "La Reforma Agraria Boliviana: Sus Antecedentes, Fundamentos, Aplicaciones y Resultados." *Re-*

vista Interamericana de Ciencias Sociales (Washington, D. C.), Vol. 2, No. 1 (1963), pp. 78-151.

Flores, Edmundo, "Land Reform in Bolivia." *Land Economics* (Madison, Wisconsin), Vol. XXX, No. 2 (May, 1954), pp. 112-124.

Flores Moncayo, José, *Derecho Agrario Boliviano*. La Paz: Editorial Don Bosco, 1956.

Ford, Thomas R., *Man and Land in Peru*. Gainesville: University of Florida Press, 1955.

Franco Barbier, Alberto, "Distribución de Tierras y Reforma Agraria." *Revista del Banco de la República* (Colombia), Vol. XXXV, No. 421 (1962), pp. 1371-1376.

Freitas Marcondes, J. V., "Reforma Agrária à Luz das Ciências Sociais." *Sociologia* (São Paulo), Vol. XXIV, No. 4 (1962), pp. 273-290.

———— *Revisão e Reforma Agrária (Quatro Estudos)*. São Paulo: Instituto dos Advogados de São Paulo, 1962.

Frigerio, Reinaldo A., *La Reforma Agraria*. Buenos Aires: Ed. Clase Obrera, 1953.

Fuentes Mohr, A., "Land Settlement and Agrarian Reform in Guatemala." *International Journal of Agrarian Affairs* (London), Vol. II, No. 1 (January, 1955), pp. 26-36.

Gay, Leslie N., "Problems of Land Ownership in Latin America." *Journal of Farm Economics* (Menasha, Wisconsin), Vol. XXXII, No. 2 (May, 1950), pp. 258-270.

Giménez Landínez, V. M., *Reforma Agraria y Desarrollo Agropecuario en Venezuela, 1959/63*. Caracas: Editorial Arte, 1963.

———— *Agricultura, Reforma Agraria y Desarrollo*. Caracas: Editorial Arte, 1962.

———— *Objetivos y Exigencias de una Reforma Agraria Integral (Objectives and Requirements of an Integral Agrarian Reform)*. Caracas: Empresa el Cojo, 1962.

Giovanni Brunoir, Pier, " 'Familiarización' e 'Industrialización' de la Estructura Agraria en América." *Revista Interamericana de Ciencias Sociales*, Vol. 2, No. 1 (1963), pp. 1-4.

Glade, William, "Social Backwardness, Social Reform, and Productivity in Latin America." *Inter-American Eco-*

nomic Affairs (Washington, D. C.), Vol. XV, No. 3 (Winter, 1961), pp. 3-32.

Gonçalves de Souza, João, "Aspects of Land Tenure Problems in Latin America." *Rural Sociology*, Vol. XXV, No. 1 (March, 1960), pp. 26-37.

Guardia Mayorga, César, *La Reforma Agraria en el Peru*. Lima: Editorial "Minka," 1957.

Hamuy, Eduardo, *Consideraciones Sociológicas en Torno a la Reforma Agraria en Latino América*. Santiago: Instituto de Sociología, Universidad de Chile, 1959.

Heath, Dwight Braley, "Commercial Agriculture and Land Reform in the Bolivian Oriente." *Inter-American Economic Affairs* (Washington, D. C.), Vol. XIII, No. 2 (Autumn, 1959), pp. 35-45.

——— "Land Reform in Bolivia." *Inter-American Economic Affairs* (Washington, D. C.), Vol. XII, No. 4 (Spring, 1959), pp. 2-26.

——— "Land Tenure and Social Organization: An Ethnohistorical Study from the Bolivian Oriente." *Inter-American Economic Affairs* (Washington, D. C.), Vol. XIII, No. 4 (Spring, 1960), pp. 46-66.

Heysen, Luis E., "Acerca de la Reforma Agraria." *Revista Mexicana de Sociología* (México), Vol. XVIII, No. 1 (Enero-Abril, 1956), pp. 97-111.

Hildebrand, John R., "Latin American Economic Development, Land Reform and U. S. Aid with Special Reference to Guatemala." *Journal of Inter-American Studies* (Gainesville, Fla.), Vol. IV, No. 3 (July, 1962), pp. 351-356.

Hill, George, Gregorio Beltrán, and Cristina Marino, "Social Welfare and Land Tenure in the Agrarian Reform Program of Venezuela." *Land Economics*, Vol. XXVIII, No. 2 (1952), pp. 17-29.

Hill, George W., and Marion T. Loftin, *Characteristics of Rural Life and the Agrarian Reform in Honduras*. Tegucigalpa: OEA Misión de Asistencia Técnica, 1961.

Hirschman, Albert O., *Journeys toward Progress*. New York: The Twentieth Century Fund, 1963, Chap. 2.

Horne, Bernardino, *Nuestro Problema Agrario*. Buenos Aires: Bernabé y Cia., 1937.

——— *Reformas Agrarias en América y en Europa*. Buenos Aires: Editorial Claridad, 1938.

Instituto Colombiano de la Reforma Agraria, *Recomendaciones sobre Política Agraria para Colombia*. Bogotá: Imprenta Nacional, 1963.

Inter-American Committee for Agricultural Development, *Meeting of High Level Experts in Agricultural Problems Held in Washington, D. C., October 9-13, 1961: Report and Official Documents of the Meeting*. Washington: Pan American Union, 1962, pp. 16-23 and 71-74.

Inter-American Development Bank, *Social Progress Trust Fund—Second Annual Report*, 1962. Washington, D. C., Inter-American Development Bank, 1963, pp. 122-131.

Julião, Francisco, *Que São as Ligas Camponesas?* Rio de Janeiro: Editôra Civilização Brasileira, 1962.

Leonard, Olen E., *Bolivia: Land, People and Institutions*. Washington, D. C.: The Scarecrow Press, 1952.

——— *Santa Cruz: Estudio Económico-Social de una Región*. La Paz: Ministerio de Agricultura, Ganadería y Colonización, 1948.

Lleras Restrepo, C., A. López Michelsen, L. Currie, and others, *Tierra. Diez Ensayos sobre la Reforma Agraria en Colombia*. Bogotá: Edición Tercer Mundo, 1961.

Loomis, C. P., and F. C. McKinney, "Systematic Differences Between Latin-American Communities of Family Farms and Large Estates." *American Journal of Sociology*, Vol. 61, No. 5 (March, 1956), pp. 404-412.

McBride, George M., *Chile: Land and Society*. New York: American Geographical Society, Research Series, 1936.

——— *Land Systems of Mexico*. New York: American Geographical Society, Research Series, No. 12, 1923.

Maddox, James S., *Land Reform in Mexico*. New York: American Universities Field Staff, 1958.

Manzanilla Schaffer, Víctor, *La Reforma Agraria*. México: Departamento de Asuntos Agrarios y Colonización, 1964.

Martínez Viademonte, Hugo, "Reforma Agraria en América. Demagogia o Necesidad?" *Cuadernos Hispano-Americanos* (Madrid), Vol. 48, No. 143 (Noviembre, 1961), pp. 225-234.

Martins, Renato Gonçalves, A *Questão Agrária e o Problema do Campônes: Fundamentos para uma Nova Política do Campo*. Rio de Janeiro: Casa do Estudante do Brasil, 1955.

Mayer, Antonio de Castro, and others, *Reforma Agrária: Questão de Consciência*. São Paulo: Editora Vera Cruz, 1961.

Mears, Leon G., "Cuba's Agriculture: Four Years under the Revolutionary Regime." *Foreign Agriculture* (Washington, D. C.), Vol. I, No. 1 (1963), pp. 4-6.

Mendieta y Núñez, Lucio, *Efectos Sociales de la Reforma Agraria en Tres Comunidades Ejidales de la República Mexicana*. México: Universidad Nacional Autónoma de México, 1960.

———— "Efectos Sociales de los Cambios en la Organización Agraria." *Revista Mexicana de Sociología* (México), Vol. XXIII, No. 2 (Mayo-Agosto, 1961), pp. 350-384.

———— "The Balance of Agrarian Reform." *Annals of the American Academy of Political and Social Sciences* (Washington, D. C.), No. 208 (March, 1940), pp. 121-131.

———— *El Problema Agrario de México*, 7th ed. México: Porrua, 1959.

———— "La Propiedad de la Tierra." *Journal of Inter-American Studies* (Gainesville, Fla.), Vol. III, No. 1 (January, 1961), pp. 27-40.

———— *La Reforma Agraria de la América Latina en Washington*. México: Instituto de Investigaciones Sociales de la Universidad Nacional Autónoma de México, 1960.

Merchán C., Antonio, "Algunos Aspectos Sociales de la Realidad Agraria Venezolana," in *Memoria: VI Congreso Latinoamericano de Sociología*, Tomo II. Caracas: Imprenta Nacional, 1961, pp. 181-222.

Monteforte Toledo, M., "La Reforma Agraria en Guatemala." *El Trimestre Económico* (México), Vol. XIX, No. 75 (1952), pp. 389-407.

Morales Benítez, Otto, *Reforma Agraria: Colombia Campesina*. Bogotá: Imprenta Nacional, 1962.

Nelson, Lowry, *Rural Cuba*. Minneapolis: University of Minnesota Press, 1950.

———— *Some Social Aspects of Agrarian Reform in Mexico, Bolivia and Venezuela* (Mimeographed). Washington, D. C.: Pan American Union, 1964.

Oliveira, Franklin de, *Que E a Revolução Brasileira?* Rio de Janeiro: Editora Civilização Brasileira, 1963.

Organization of American States–Pan American Union, General Secretariat, *Plantation Systems of the New World* (Social Science Monographs, VII). Washington, D. C.: Pan American Union, 1959.

Ortiz Villacís, Marcelo, *La Administración en el Proceso de la Reforma Agraria*. Quito: Instituto Nacional de Colonización, 1964.

Paredes Moreira, José Luis, *Causas e Efectos de la Reforma Agraria en Guatemala* (Mimeographed). Guatemala City: Instituto de Investigaciones Económicas y Sociales, Universidad de San Carlos de Guatemala, 1961.

Parsons, James J., *Antioqueño Colonization in Western Colombia* (Ibero-Americana, Vol. XXXII). Berkeley and Los Angeles: University of California Press, 1949.

Parsons, Kenneth H., Raymond J. Penn, and Philip M. Raup, eds., *Land Tenure: Proceedings of the International Conference on Land Tenure and Related Problems in World Agriculture Held at Madison, Wisconsin, 1951*. Madison: University of Wisconsin Press, 1956.

Patch, Richard W., "Bolivia: U. S. Assistance in a Revolutionary Setting," in Philip E. Mosely, ed., *Social Change in Latin America Today*. New York: Harper and Brothers, 1960.

Penn, Raymond J., and Jorge Schuster, "La Reforma Agraria de Venezuela." *Revista Interamericana de Ciencias Sociales*, Vol. 2, No. 1 (1963), pp. 29-39.

Peru, Comisión para la Reforma Agraria y la Vivienda, in *La Reforma Agraria en el Peru: Exposición de Motivos y Projecto de Ley*. Lima: Talleres Gráficos P. L. Villanueva, S. A., 1960.

204)   AGRARIAN REFORM IN LATIN AMERICA

Pino Navarro, Arturo, *La Tenencia de la Tierra y la Reforma Agraria en Honduras.* Tegucigalpa: OEA, Misión de Asistencia Técnica, 1961.

Poblete Troncosco, Moisés, *La Reforma Agraria en América Latina.* Santiago: Editorial Andrés Bello, 1961.

Prado, Caio, Jr., "Contribuição para a Análise da Questão Agrária no Brasil." *Revista Brasiliense* (São Paulo), No. 28 (Março-Abril, 1960), pp. 163-238.

Rangel, Inacio, *Questão Agrária Brasileira.* Rio de Janeiro: Presidência da República, Conselho do Desenvolvimento, 1961.

Reale, Miguel, *Diretrizes da Política Agrária Paulista.* São Paulo: Imprensa Oficial do Estado, 1963.

Reyes Osorio, Sergio, "La Reforma Agraria: Sus Exitos y Fracasos." *Boletín de Estudios Especiales* (México: Banco Nacional de Crédito Ejidal), Vol. X, No. 112 (February, 1958), pp. 65-70.

Rios, José Arthur, "O Que É e não É Reforma Agrária." *Cadernos Brasileiros* (Rio de Janeiro), Ano V, No. 4 (Julho-Agósto, 1963), pp. 45-50.

———— "Rumos da Reforma Agrária." *Arquivos de Direito Social* (São Paulo), Vol. 10, No. 1 (1952), pp. 3-18.

———— ed., *Recomendações sôbre Reforma Agrária.* Rio de Janeiro: Instituto Brasileiro de Ação Democrática, 1961.

Royal Institute of International Affairs, "The Indian and the Land in Latin America." *The World Today* (London), Vol. X, No. 10 (October, 1954), pp. 447-457.

Saunders, John Van Dyke, "Man-Land Relations in Ecuador." *Rural Sociology,* Vol. XXVI, No. 1 (March, 1961), pp. 57-69.

Schilling, Paulo R., *O Que é Reforma Agrária?* Rio de Janeiro: Editora Civilização Brasileira, 1963.

Schulman, Sam, "The Colono System in Latin America." *Rural Sociology,* Vol. XX, No. 1 (March, 1955), pp. 34-40.

Senior, Clarence, *Land Reform and Democracy.* Gainesville: University of Florida Press, 1958.

Silva Herzog, Jesús, *El Agrarismo Mexicano y la Reforma Agraria.* México: Fondo de Cultura Económica, 1959.

Simpson, E. N.: *The Ejido: Mexico's Way Out*. Chapel Hill: University of North Carolina Press, 1937.

Smith, T. Lynn, "Algumas Considerações sôbre o Estatuto da Lavoura Canavieira." *Jurídica* (Rio de Janeiro), Ano IX, Vol. XXVIII, No. 82 (Julho-Setembro, 1963), pp. 297-308.

———— "Aspectos Fundamentales de la Reforma Agraria." *Cuadernos* (Paris), No. 55 (December, 1961), pp. 28-34.

———— *Brazil: People and Institutions*, 3rd ed. Baton Rouge: Louisiana State University Press, 1963. Chaps. 12, 13, 14, and 15.

———— *Current Social Trends and Problems in Latin America* (Latin American Monographs No. 1). Gainesville: University of Florida Press, 1957, Chap. 3.

———— *Sociología Rural*. Maracaibo, Venezuela: Universidad del Zulia, 1963, pp. 83-93, 111-132.

———— *Sociología Rural: la Comunidad y la Reforma Agraria* (Monografías Sociologícas No. 3). Bogotá: Universidad Nacional de Colombia, 1959.

———— "Some Observations on Land Tenure in Colombia." *Foreign Agriculture* (Washington, D. C.), Vol. XVI, No. 6 (1952), pp. 119-124.

Souza Barros, *Exodo e Fixação, Sugestões para uma Política de Colonização e Aldeamento no Nordeste*. Rio de Janeiro: Ministério de Agricultura, Serviço de Informação Agrícola, 1953.

Stark, Harry, *Social and Economic Frontiers in Latin America*. Dubuque, Iowa: Wm. C. Brown Co., 1961, Chap. 10.

Sterling, H. S., "The Emergence of the Medium-size Private Farm as the Most Successful Product of Mexico's Agrarian Reform." *Association of American Geographers Annals* (New York), Vol. XXXIX, No. 3 (March, 1949), pp. 58-59.

Tannenbaum, Frank, *The Mexican Agrarian Revolution*. New York: The Macmillan Co., 1929.

Taylor, C. C., *Rural Life in Argentina*. Baton Rouge: Louisiana State University Press, 1948.

Taylor, Paul C., *Venezuela: A Case Study of Relationships between Community Development and Agrarian Reform*.

Caracas: Bureau of Social Affairs of the United Nations, 1961.

United Nations, Food and Agriculture Organization, *Report of the Regional Land Reform Team for Latin America,* Publication No. 1388 (Mimeographed). Rome: Food and Agriculture Organization, 1961.

United Nations, Food and Agriculture Organization, and the International Labour Organization, *Progress in Land Reform: Third Report.* New York: United Nations, 1962.

Venezuela, Ministerio de Agricultura y Cria, *Ley de Reforma Agraria.* Caracas: Publicaciones Nacionales, 1960.

Vivanco, Antonino C., "Derecho Agrario y Reforma Agraria en América Latina." *Journal of Inter-American Studies* (Gainesville, Fla.), Vol. IV, No. 2 (April, 1962), pp. 233-245.

Weeks, David, "European Antecedents of Land Tenure and Agrarian Organization of Hispanic America." *Journal of Land and Public Utility Economics* (Madison, Wisconsin), Vol. XXIII, No. 2 (May, 1947), pp. 153-168.

———— "Land Tenure in Bolivia." *Journal of Land and Public Utility Economics* (Madison, Wisconsin), Vol. XXIII, No. 3 (August, 1947), pp. 321-336.

Whetten, Nathan L., *Guatemala, The Land and the People.* New Haven: Yale University Press, 1961.

———— "Land Reform in a Modern World." *Rural Sociology,* Vol. XIX, No. 4 (December, 1954), pp. 329-337.

———— *Rural Mexico.* Chicago: University of Chicago Press, 1948.

BORZOI BOOKS ON LATIN AMERICA

Under the general editorship of Lewis Hanke,
UNIVERSITY OF CALIFORNIA, IRVINE

* Also available in a hardbound edition

A NOTE ON THE TYPE

This book is set in Electra, a Linotype face designed by W. A. Dwiggins. This face cannot be classified as either modern or old-style. It is not based on any historical model, nor does it echo any particular period or style. It avoids the extreme contrasts between thick and thin elements that mark most modern faces, and attempts to give a feeling of fluidity, power, and speed.